The Books of Enoch Collection

Discover the Complete Narrative of These Hidden Texts Including the Fallen Angels, Watchers, Nephilim and More

Zarek Altheon

Copyright © 2025 by Zarek Altheon
All rights reserved.

No part of this book may be reproduced, stored in a retrieval system, or transmitted in any form or by any means, electronic, mechanical, photocopying, recording, or otherwise, without the prior written permission of the author, except for brief quotations used in reviews or scholarly works.

Contents

Introduction 1

The Book of Watchers – Enoch's Ethiopic Book 1 4

The Book Of Noah – Apocryphal Part Of Noah's Book Excluded From Canonical Bible 66

The Book of the Luminaries of the Heaven – Enoch's Ethiopic Book 3 87

The Book of Dreams and Visions – Enoch's Ethiopic Book 4 107

The Epistle of Enoch – The Ethiopic Book of Enoch (Book 5) 125

Introduction

The term *Apocrypha* refers to a collection of ancient religious writings that, for various reasons, were excluded from the canonical scriptures of most mainstream religious traditions, particularly the Jewish and Christian faiths. The word *apocrypha* itself comes from the Greek word ἀπόκρυφος (*apokryphos*), meaning "hidden" or "secret." This suggests that these texts were once considered too obscure, controversial, or mysterious for inclusion in the accepted canon of scripture.

Though often overlooked or misunderstood, the Apocryphal books play a crucial role in shedding light on the beliefs, customs, and theological developments of the ancient world. The Apocrypha consists of writings that were either written during the intertestamental period (the time between the Old and New Testaments), or were later works that were once revered but gradually fell out of favor.

These texts cover a wide range of themes, from historical narratives to visions of the divine, from ethical teachings to apocalyptic revelations. Many of the Apocryphal works offer deeper insights into

Jewish thought, including stories that were highly influential during the time of Jesus and early Christianity. While some of these writings were accepted by certain early Christian communities, they were ultimately excluded from the official Bible due to concerns over authorship, authenticity, and theological disagreements.

Among the most significant of these Apocryphal writings are the *Books of Enoch*, a series of ancient texts that expand upon the enigmatic figure of Enoch, the great-grandfather of Noah, who is mentioned briefly in the Hebrew Bible. These books, particularly *1 Enoch*, *2 Enoch*, and *3 Enoch*, delve into the cosmic mysteries of angels, the Watchers, the Nephilim, and the unfolding of divine judgment.

The *Books of Enoch* stand as a powerful testament to the complexities of early Jewish apocalyptic thought, revealing a world where the boundaries between the divine and human realms were fluid, and the consequences of heavenly rebellion were far-reaching. They offer a window into a worldview where fallen angels, or *Watchers*, descend to Earth, corrupt humanity, and birth the Nephilim, a race of giants. These tales were not only thought-provoking but also served as moral warnings, calling for righteousness and reverence to the divine.

The fascinating narratives of the *Books of Enoch* were so influential that they inspired later Christian and Jewish mysticism, shaping theological concepts like the nature of sin, the role of angels, and the coming of a messianic savior. Despite their exclusion from the modern Bible, these writings continue to stir the imagination of scholars, theologians, and readers alike, offering a unique glimpse into ancient beliefs and the ever-evolving understanding of the cosmos.

The Book of Watchers – Enoch's Ethiopic Book 1

Chapter 1

1. Who will remain when the time of tribulation arrives, and the wicked and godless are taken away?
2. Enoch, a man of righteousness, blessed with divine vision, began to experience his revelation. He saw the Holy One in the heavens, as revealed by the angels, comprehending everything they showed him—not for the people of his time, but for a future generation yet to come.
3. He spoke of the chosen ones and delivered a parable concerning them: The Holy Great One will emerge from His dwelling.
4. The eternal God will set foot upon the earth, even upon Mount Sinai, displaying His power as He descends from the heavens.
5. Fear will seize all, and the watchers will tremble. A profound terror will spread over the earth.

6. The highest mountains will quake, and the tallest hills will be brought low, melting as wax melts before the flame.
7. The earth itself will crack open, and everything upon it will be destroyed, for judgment will descend upon all mankind.
8. Yet, the righteous will find peace, as He will offer mercy to the elect. They will belong to God, thrive, be blessed, and receive His aid, with light shining upon them as He grants them His peace.
9. Behold! He comes with ten thousand of His holy ones to bring judgment upon all, to obliterate the ungodly, and to convict all flesh for their acts of wickedness and the harsh words they spoke against Him.

Chapter 2

1. Observe the heavens and see how everything follows its prescribed course, with the celestial bodies rising and setting in their appointed times without deviation.
2. Do not disrupt the natural order they follow. Look upon the earth and see how it remains firm, from the beginning to the end, unchanged and enduring.

3. Consider the works of God all around you. See how the earth is nourished by water in every season, with clouds, dew, and rain providing sustenance year-round.

Chapter 3

1. Observe how, in the cold of winter, the trees appear barren, their leaves fallen away—except for a few trees that retain their foliage for two or three years before new leaves take their place.

Chapter 4

1. Watch the summer days as the sun blazes overhead,
2. Causing people to seek shelter from its scorching rays. The ground becomes so heated that walking on it or even on a rock is unbearable due to the intense warmth.

Chapter 5

1. See how the trees cover themselves in green leaves and bear fruit. Take note of all His works, and recognize that the Eternal One has made them this way.
2. All His creations continue their tasks year

after year without change, fulfilling what God has ordained.
3. The sea and rivers perform their duties and do not stray from His commands.
4. Yet, you have not been steadfast, nor followed the Lord's commands. Instead, you have turned away, speaking proud and hard words with impure mouths against His greatness.
5. Hard-hearted ones, you will find no peace. You will curse your days, and the years of your life will vanish, multiplying in eternal condemnation with no mercy for you.
6. In that time, your name will become an everlasting curse to the righteous. Through you, all who curse will curse, and the godless will be cursed because of you.
7. Joy and forgiveness of sins will come to the righteous, with mercy, peace, and patience. Salvation will come to them, a beautiful light.
8. But for all sinners, there will be no salvation; instead, a curse will remain upon you.
9. For the chosen, there will be light, joy, and peace, and they will inherit the earth.
10. Wisdom will be granted to the elect, and

they will live without sin, neither through ungodliness nor pride; the wise will remain humble.

11. They will not sin again, nor transgress all their days, nor die from divine anger or wrath. They will complete their allotted days in peace,

12. And their lives will lengthen in joy, with their years multiplying in eternal gladness and peace, all their days.

Chapter 6

1. As the human population grew, during those times, beautiful daughters were born to them.
2. The angels, the sons of heaven, looked upon these daughters and were filled with desire, saying to one another, "Let us take wives from among the daughters of men,
3. And father children by them." Semjaza, their leader, then said,
4. "I fear that you may not all consent to this, and I alone will bear the consequences for such a great sin."
5. But they all answered, "Let us swear an oath and bind ourselves with a mutual curse,

6. To carry out this plan and not abandon it." Together, they all swore, binding themselves with a solemn oath.
7. There were two hundred of them in total who descended in the days of Jared, to the peak of Mount Hermon, which was named for the oath they took
8. And for the curse they bound themselves with on that mountain.
9. Their leaders included: Samlazaz, their chief, along with Araklba, Rameel, Kokablel, Tamlel, Ramlel, Danel, Ezeqeel, Baraqijal,
10. Asael, Armaros, Batarel, Ananel, Zaqiel, Samsapeel, Satarel, Turel, Jomjael, and Sariel. These were the heads of groups of ten.

Chapter 7

1. Afterward, the other angels took wives, each choosing one for themselves, and they lived with them, defiling their bodies and teaching them various magical arts.
2. They instructed them in charms, enchantments, and the art of root-cutting, as

well as sharing knowledge of the uses of plants.
3. The women conceived and bore mighty giants, towering at three thousand cubits in height.
4. These giants consumed all the resources of humanity, and when there was no more food to sustain them, they turned on mankind.
5. They began to devour humans, feeding on their flesh.
6. Their sins extended to harming birds, animals, reptiles, and fish, as they feasted on one another's flesh and drank their blood.
7. In response, the earth raised an accusation against these lawless beings.

Chapter 8

1. Azazel introduced humanity to the art of crafting weapons, including swords, knives, shields, and breastplates. He revealed how to work with metals, creating bracelets, ornaments, and even taught the use of antimony. He showed them how to beautify their eyelids, apply precious stones,
2. And use coloring tinctures. This led to widespread corruption as wickedness

flourished, and people engaged in immoral acts,
3. Becoming increasingly corrupt in all their ways. Semjaza imparted the knowledge of enchantments and root-cutting; Armaros taught how to break enchantments; Baraqijal shared the wisdom of astrology; Kokabel taught about the constellations; Ezeqeel instructed on cloud lore; Araqiel taught about earth signs; Shamsiel explained the signs of the sun, and Sariel taught the movement of the moon. As destruction spread, the people cried out, and their pleas reached the heavens.

Chapter 9

1. Michael, Uriel, Raphael, and Gabriel looked down from the heavens,
2. And observed the bloodshed and rampant lawlessness on the earth. They conversed with each other, saying, "The earth, desolate and voiceless, cries out, raising its lament to the gates of heaven.
3. And now, the holy ones in heaven, the souls of humanity, bring their plea, saying, 'Present our case before the Most High.'
4. They spoke to the Lord of ages, saying, 'Lord of lords, God of gods, King of kings, and God

of the ages, Your throne of glory stands eternal,

5. And Your name is holy, magnificent, and blessed for all eternity! You created everything and have dominion over all. All things are open to You, and You see all things;
6. Nothing is hidden from You. You observe the deeds of Azazel, who has led humanity into sin and uncovered the eternal secrets kept in heaven,
7. Secrets that humanity sought to uncover. And Semjaza, whom You placed in charge of his companions,
8. Has gone to the daughters of men, defiling himself and teaching them all manner of sin. The women have borne giants,
9. And the earth is filled with bloodshed and wickedness.
10. Now, the souls of the deceased cry out, their pleas reaching the heavens, unable to cease due to the lawlessness on earth.
11. You know everything before it happens, and You see these actions but allow them to unfold. You have not told us what we should do about these matters.'"

Chapter 10

1. Then the Most High, the Holy and Mighty One, spoke and sent Uriel to the son of Lamech,
2. Saying, "Go to Noah and deliver My message: 'Take refuge and prepare yourself, for the end is near. The earth will be laid waste, and a great flood will cover it,
3. Wiping out all that dwells upon it. Instruct him to find safety,
4. So that his offspring may survive and carry on for generations to come.'" Then the Lord spoke to Raphael, saying, "Seize Azazel, bind him hand and foot, and cast him into the darkness. Open a chasm in the desolate land,
5. In Dudael, and hurl him into it. Cover him with sharp stones and utter darkness, ensuring he sees no light again."
6. On the appointed day of final judgment, he will be cast into the flames.
7. Purify the earth, which has been defiled by the fallen angels, and declare its restoration so that the plague may end, preventing humanity from perishing due to the

knowledge the Watchers revealed to their descendants.
8. Let all wrongdoing be placed upon Azazel.
9. Then the Lord spoke to Gabriel, saying, "Take action against the offspring of the fallen and the wicked, those born in sin. Cause them to turn against each other in battle, leading to their own destruction.
10. Their lives will be cut short. No plea on their behalf will be heard, for their fathers had hoped for them to live eternally."
11. They believed they would live for five hundred years. Then the Lord said to Michael, "Go and restrain Semjaza and those who followed him in corruption,
12. Along with them in their defilement. When their offspring have destroyed one another, and they witness the downfall of those they cherished, imprison them for seventy generations in the depths of the earth, until the day of judgment and their final condemnation.
13. They will be cast into the abyss of fire,
14. To suffer torment and imprisonment for eternity. Those sentenced with them will remain bound for all future generations.

15. Eradicate the spirits of the wicked and the descendants of the fallen Watchers."
16. For they have brought harm upon humanity. Let all wickedness come to an end so that righteousness and truth may flourish, bringing blessings. The deeds of the righteous will lead to lasting joy and peace.
17. The righteous will be delivered and will live to bring forth countless descendants, completing their lives in peace, both in youth and old age.
18. The entire earth will be cultivated in righteousness, covered with trees and filled with abundance.
19. Fruit-bearing trees will be planted, vineyards will yield plentiful wine, and sown seeds will produce a thousandfold. Each measure of olives will yield ten presses of oil.
20. Purge the earth of oppression, sin, and wickedness, removing all impurity. Humanity will become righteous,
21. And all nations will worship and praise My name. The earth will be purified from defilement, sin, punishment, and suffering, and never again will such afflictions be brought upon it for all generations to come."

Chapter 11

1. In that time, I will open the heavenly storehouses of blessings,
2. Pouring them upon the earth for the toil and labor of humanity. Truth and peace will be joined together, remaining throughout all generations.

Chapter 12

1. Before these events, Enoch was taken away, and no one among humankind knew where he was—
2. His dwelling place or what had become of him. His purpose was with the Watchers, and he spent his days among the holy ones.
3. And I, Enoch, gave praise to the Lord of majesty and the King of all ages. Suddenly,
4. The Watchers called upon me—Enoch, the scribe—and said, "Enoch, recorder of righteousness, go and deliver a message to the Watchers of heaven who abandoned their sacred and eternal place,
5. Defiling themselves with women and behaving like mortals, taking wives for

themselves. 'You have brought great ruin upon the earth, and for you, there will be neither peace nor forgiveness of sin.
6. Though you cherish your children, you will see their destruction and mourn over them. You will cry out forever, but neither mercy nor peace will be granted to you.'"

Chapter 13

1. Enoch went forth and declared, "Azazel, no peace shall be granted to you. A severe judgment has been pronounced,
2. Binding you in chains. You will receive no leniency, nor will your pleas be heard, for the corruption and godlessness you have introduced,
3. The sin and transgression you have taught humanity." Then I addressed all of them together,
4. And fear overtook them; they trembled, overcome with dread. They pleaded with me to compose a petition on their behalf, seeking mercy, and to present their request before the Lord of heaven.
5. From that moment, they could no longer speak to Him or lift their eyes to the heavens,

overwhelmed with shame for their sins and the judgment upon them. I recorded their plea, including prayers concerning their spirits and actions, documenting each request separately as they sought forgiveness and an extension of their days.

6. Then I departed and sat by the waters of Dan, in the land of Dan, to the south and west of Mount Hermon, reading their petition until I fell asleep.
7. In my sleep, a dream came to me, and visions unfolded before my eyes. I saw scenes of judgment, and a voice commanded me to share these visions with the sons of heaven and to reprimand them.
8. When I awoke, I went to them and found them gathered, mourning at Abelsjail,
9. Between Lebanon and Seneser, their faces were covered in sorrow. I recounted to them all the visions I had seen in my dream, and I began to speak words of righteousness, rebuking the heavenly Watchers.

Chapter 14

1. This is the record of the words of righteousness and the rebuke of the Watchers,
2. Given by command of the Holy and Mighty One, revealed through a vision. In my dream, I saw with a human understanding—bestowed upon me by the Great One—so that I could comprehend and communicate wisdom.
3. Just as He has given wisdom to humankind, He enabled me to deliver this admonition to the Watchers,
4. The sons of heaven. I recorded your plea, but in my vision, I saw that it would not be granted.
5. A judgment had already been decreed, and you would not be allowed to return to heaven; your exile to the earth is permanent.
6. Before that time comes, you will witness the downfall of your beloved sons and find no joy in them, for they will perish by the sword.
7. Your petition on their behalf will not be accepted, nor will your own, regardless of your supplications, prayers, or the words I have inscribed.
8. In my vision, I was surrounded by clouds, drawn in by a thick mist, and propelled

forward by flashing stars and streaks of lightning.
9. Powerful winds lifted me, carrying me upward into the heavens. I arrived at a towering wall made of crystal, encircled by tongues of fire, and a deep fear overtook me.
10. As I moved through the flames, I approached a magnificent house of crystal. Its walls gleamed like a mosaic of shimmering stones, and its foundation was entirely made of crystal.
11. Above me, the ceiling resembled the movement of stars and lightning, adorned with fiery cherubim, while the sky above was as clear as flowing water. A blazing fire enveloped the walls, and the doors shone with intense flames.
12. As I stepped inside, I felt the overwhelming contrast of scorching heat and piercing cold.
13. No comfort or joy dwelled within—only a deep sense of awe and trembling overtook me.
14. Shaken to my core, I fell prostrate in reverence.
15. Then, I beheld another house, even greater than the first,

16. Its entrance wide open, burning with a consuming fire. The sheer splendor and vastness of this place were beyond words.
17. The ground beneath was ablaze with fire, while above, lightning and stars illuminated the expanse.
18. The ceiling, too, was engulfed in flames, and at the center stood a magnificent throne, shining like crystal. Its wheels radiated with brilliance like the sun, and visions of cherubim surrounded it.
19. Streams of blazing fire flowed from beneath the throne, their intensity making it impossible to look upon.
20. Seated upon the throne was the Great Glory, His garments radiating a brightness surpassing the sun, whiter than the purest snow.
21. No angel could enter His presence, nor could any being gaze upon His face due to the overwhelming splendor and majesty.
22. A barrier of fire encircled Him, with a mighty blaze burning before Him, allowing none to draw near. Multitudes beyond measure, ten thousand times ten thousand, stood in attendance,

23. Yet He required no counsel, for the holiest ones remained ever at His side, never straying.
24. As I lay prostrate, trembling before Him, I heard His voice calling to me, saying, "Come forward, Enoch, and hear My words."
25. One of the holy ones reached out, lifting me up and guiding me toward the entrance, where I bowed my face in reverence.

Chapter 15

1. He spoke, and I heard His voice, saying, "Do not be afraid, Enoch, you who are righteous and a scribe of truth.
2. Come closer and listen to My words. Go and deliver this message to the Watchers of heaven who sent you to intercede on their behalf: 'It is not for men to plead for angels, but for angels to intercede for men.'
3. Why did you abandon the holy, eternal heavens and defile yourselves with the daughters of men? Why did you take human wives, acting like those born of the earth and fathering giants?

4. You, who were once pure, spiritual beings, meant to live eternally, have polluted yourselves with the blood of women, craving flesh as mortals do, though you were never destined to perish as they do.
5. I gave mankind wives so that they might bear children and continue their existence on earth.
6. But you were created as spiritual beings, meant to live forever, not bound by the limitations of mortal flesh.
7. That is why I never appointed wives for you, for those who dwell in heaven are meant to remain in heaven.
8. Now, because the giants are born of both spirit and flesh, they will be known as evil spirits upon the earth, and they will remain here.
9. Their spirits will not ascend to heaven, for they are neither fully of heaven nor fully of earth. Instead, they will be bound to the earth as wandering spirits of wickedness.
10. The domain of heavenly beings is the heavens, but the spirits of the giants, having originated from a corrupted union, shall remain upon the earth forever.

11. These spirits will bring suffering, oppression, destruction, and war. They will torment mankind, stirring up strife and hardship, forever restless and unsatisfied.
12. Though they do not eat, they will hunger; though they cannot drink, they will thirst, and they will become a source of corruption. These spirits will turn against humanity and the women from whom they were born."

Chapter 16

1. From the time the giants perished and their bodies decayed, their spirits emerged, bringing destruction upon the earth without restraint. These spirits will continue their influence until the final day—when the great judgment arrives, marking the end of this age,
2. Bringing eternal judgment upon the Watchers and the wicked. To the Watchers who sent you to plead for them, deliver this message:
3. "Though you once dwelled in the heavens, your knowledge was incomplete. The little wisdom you possessed, you shared with women, and through this, great corruption spread upon the earth."

4. Therefore, tell them, 'You will never find peace.'"

Chapter 17

1. They led me to a place where those present blazed like flames of fire,
2. Yet could take on human form at will. They guided me into a realm of deep darkness and to a towering mountain that reached the heavens.
3. There, I saw the domains of the celestial lights and the vast storehouses of stars and thunder, hidden within the deepest depths.
4. I beheld a fiery bow, arrows, a quiver, a sword of flames, and bolts of lightning. They led me to the waters that grant life,
5. And to the western fire, where the sun descends at the close of the day.
6. I arrived at a river of fire, its flames flowing like water, pouring into a great sea in the west. I beheld mighty rivers and reached an immense current in a place of profound darkness,
7. A region untouched by any living being. I saw the mountains cloaked in winter's shadow and the source

8. From which the waters of the abyss emerge. I gazed upon the mouths of every earthly river and the opening of the great abyss.

Chapter 18

1. I observed the vast storehouses of the winds and how the Most High set them in place,
2. Establishing them to sustain creation and lay the foundation of the earth. I saw the cornerstone upon which the world rests and the four winds
3. That uphold both the earth and the expanse of the heavens. I witnessed the winds that stretch out the heavenly vault, stationed between the sky and the earth as pillars of the heavens.
4. I beheld the winds of the heavens turning in their courses, directing the sun
5. And guiding the stars to their appointed places. I saw the earthly winds that carry the clouds, and I walked the paths traversed by the angels.
6. At the very edges of the earth, I gazed upon the firmament above. Moving forward, I came upon a place that burned both day and

night, where seven towering mountains stood, made of precious stones.
7. Three of these were positioned towards the east and three to the south. The mountains in the east displayed magnificent hues—one of radiant stone, one of pearl, and one of brilliant jacinth. The southern mountains glowed with deep red stone.
8. The central mountain reached into the heavens, resembling the very throne of the Almighty, its base of pure alabaster and its peak shining like sapphire.
9. There, I saw an unceasing blaze of fire.
10. Beyond these mountains lay the boundary where the earth reaches its end, and the heavens are brought to completion.
11. I discovered a vast abyss, filled with columns of celestial fire, with flames descending into its depths, extending beyond all measure in height and depth.
12. Beyond this abyss lay a realm where neither the sky above nor solid ground below could be found—no water,
13. No birds, only an immense, barren, and terrifying expanse. There, I beheld seven stars glowing like burning mountains.

14. When I asked about them, the angel answered, "This marks the boundary of the heavens and the earth; it has become the place of imprisonment for these stars and the celestial hosts.
15. These stars, which wander in the fire, have defied the commands of the Most High from the moment of their rising,
16. Failing to appear in their appointed times. In His wrath, He has bound them here until the completion of their judgment, for ten thousand years."

Chapter 19

1. Uriel spoke to me, saying, "Here are the angels who abandoned their place in heaven and took human wives, corrupting themselves. Their spirits, having taken on various forms, misled humankind, causing them to revere false gods and worship demons. Here they shall remain, bound until the day of the great judgment,
2. When they will face their final condemnation. Their punishment will last until the appointed time of their destruction. As for the women

3. Who were led astray by them, they shall be transformed into sirens." I, Enoch, was the only one who saw this vision of the fate that awaits all things, a vision that no other has seen as I have.

Chapter 20

1. These are the names of the holy angels who have been appointed as guardians.
2. Uriel, one of the holy angels, is responsible for overseeing the world and the realm of Tartarus.
3. Raphael, another of the holy angels, is entrusted with the care of the spirits of humanity.
4. Raguel, a holy angel, executes justice upon the world of celestial bodies.
5. Michael, counted among the holy angels, is assigned to watch over the virtuous among humankind and maintain order amid chaos.
6. Saraqael, one of the holy angels, has authority over the spirits that transgress in the spiritual realm.
7. Gabriel, a holy angel, is given dominion over Paradise, as well as the serpents and the cherubim.

8. Remiel, a holy angel, is appointed by God to oversee those who will experience resurrection.

Chapter 21

1. I was led to a realm of disorder and chaos,
2. A place unlike any other, where neither heaven was above nor a stable earth beneath—only a vast, terrifying emptiness.
3. There, I saw seven celestial bodies bound together, resembling great mountains engulfed in flames.
4. I asked, "What offense led to their imprisonment, and why have they been cast into this place?"
5. Uriel, one of the holy angels accompanying me and overseeing them, responded, "Enoch, why do you seek to understand this matter?
6. These are the heavenly stars that defied the Lord's decree. They are held here in confinement until the appointed time, when their transgressions will be accounted for after ten thousand years."
7. From there, I was taken to another place, even more dreadful, where an immense fire blazed, stretching downward into the abyss,

its fiery columns descending endlessly into the depths.
8. Struck with fear, I exclaimed, "This place is beyond terrifying! Its sight alone fills me with dread!"
9. Uriel, the holy angel who was with me, turned and asked, "Enoch, why are you so afraid?"
10. I answered, "Because this place is overwhelming, and the torment within is unbearable to witness." Uriel then explained, "This is the prison for the fallen angels, where they will remain for all eternity."

Chapter 22

1. From there, I was taken to another location, where I saw a towering mountain of solid rock in the west.
2. Within this mountain were four vast, deep, and smooth hollow spaces, dark and mysterious in appearance.
3. Then Raphael, one of the holy angels accompanying me, explained, "These hollows were created to receive the spirits of the deceased,

4. So that the souls of all humanity may be gathered here. These places have been prepared to hold them until the appointed time of judgment,
5. When the great day of justice arrives." I observed the spirits of the departed, their voices rising toward heaven in lamentation.
6. I turned to Raphael and asked, "Whose spirit is this, crying out and sending its voice to the heavens?"
7. He replied, "This is the spirit of Abel, who was slain by his brother Cain. His soul continues to cry out against him, awaiting the day when Cain's descendants are removed from the earth,
8. And his lineage is forever cut off from humanity." Then I inquired about the purpose of these separate hollow places.
9. Raphael explained, "These three divisions were created to separate the spirits of the dead. The first is for the righteous, where a spring of bright water flows.
10. The second holds the spirits of sinners who were buried without receiving judgment in their lifetimes.
11. Here, they endure great suffering until the day of divine judgment, when those who

have cursed and acted wickedly will face eternal condemnation.
12. They will remain bound forever. The third division is for the spirits of those who plead for justice, exposing the destruction caused by sinners throughout history.
13. The last division is for those who were not righteous but were consumed by sin, completely immersed in wickedness. Their spirits remain here with others like them, and they will not rise again on the day of judgment nor be released from this place."
14. Then I lifted my voice in praise and said, "Blessed is the Lord of glory, the righteous ruler for all eternity."

Chapter 23

1. From there, I was taken to the westernmost edge of the earth.
2. I saw a fire that burned endlessly, never ceasing its course, neither by day nor by night.
3. Curious, I asked, "What is this fire that never stops burning?"
4. Raguel, one of the holy angels who accompanied me, answered, "This is the

perpetual flame of the west, which follows the celestial bodies on their paths."

Chapter 24

1. Next, I was led to another place on earth, where I saw an expanse of mountains continuously ablaze, their fires never extinguished.
2. Beyond this, there were seven magnificent mountains, each distinct in its beauty. The stones composing them were of brilliant splendor, creating a breathtaking and awe-inspiring sight. Three of these mountains rose in the east, stacked upon one another, and three stood in the south in a similar formation. Between them, deep, rugged valleys cut through the land, each isolated from the others.
3. At the center stood a seventh mountain, towering above the rest like a throne, surrounded by fragrant trees.
4. Among these trees, I noticed one unlike any I had ever encountered before. Its fragrance surpassed all others, and its leaves, blossoms, and wood never withered or decayed.

5. The fruit of this tree, radiant in appearance, resembled the dates of a palm. I marveled, saying, "This tree is truly beautiful and fragrant, its leaves so delightful, and its blossoms so wonderful."
6. Then Michael, one of the honored and holy angels beside me, and their leader, answered my inquiry.

Chapter 25

1. He turned to me and said, "Enoch, why are you so eager to understand the fragrance of this tree and its significance?"
2. I responded, "I wish to know everything about it, especially its purpose."
3. He replied, "This towering mountain, whose peak resembles the throne of God, is indeed where the Holy Great One, the Lord of Glory, the Eternal King, will sit when He descends in righteousness to visit the earth.
4. As for this fragrant tree, no human may touch it until the appointed day of judgment, when justice will be fulfilled, and all things will be completed forever. Then, it will be given to the righteous and holy.

5. Its fruit shall serve as nourishment for the chosen, and it will be transplanted to the sacred dwelling of the Lord, where it will remain eternally.
6. The righteous will rejoice in its presence, and its fragrance will dwell within them. They will live long lives upon the earth, just as their forefathers did, free from pain, suffering, or calamity."
7. Hearing this, I praised the God of Glory, the Eternal King, who prepared such blessings for the righteous, keeping them as gifts for His chosen ones.

Chapter 26

1. From there, I journeyed to the heart of the earth, where I came upon a blessed land filled with trees, all drawing life from a single, ever-blooming tree.
2. I saw a sacred mountain, and beneath it, on the eastern side, a stream flowed gently southward.
3. To the east of this mountain, another, even taller mountain stood, separated by a deep and narrow valley, with a stream running beneath its rocky base.

4. To the west, I beheld a smaller mountain of moderate height, and between them lay a steep, dry valley. Another deep, barren ravine stretched across the end of the three mountains.
5. These ravines were all deep and narrow, hewn from solid rock, with no trees growing within them. I marveled at their sheer depth and ruggedness, astonished by the wonder of their formation.

Chapter 27

1. Then I inquired, "What is the purpose of this land, filled with trees, and the cursed valley beside it?"
2. Uriel, one of the holy angels accompanying me, answered, "This cursed valley is reserved for those condemned forever. It is the place where all who have spoken against the Lord, uttering harsh and blasphemous words, will be gathered for their judgment.
3. In the final days, the righteous will witness the judgment carried out upon these individuals. This will happen in the presence of the righteous, and it will endure eternally.

Here, the merciful will praise the Lord of Glory, the Everlasting King.
4. As the condemned face their judgment, those whom the Lord has shown mercy will glorify Him for His justice and the judgment He has assigned."
5. Then I lifted my voice in praise to the Lord of Glory, exalting His majesty and offering Him great honor.

Chapter 28

1. From there, I journeyed eastward, entering a rugged mountain range in the desert, where I saw a solitary wilderness abundant with trees and plants.
2. Streams of water flowed from above,
3. Rushing with great force toward the northwest, creating mist and dew that spread in every direction.

Chapter 29

1. Continuing my journey, I arrived at another place in the desert, near the eastern side of the mountain range.
2. There, I discovered a grove of fragrant trees, their aroma filling the air with the scents of

frankincense and myrrh. The trees had the appearance of almond trees.

Chapter 30

1. Traveling further east, I came upon another location, a valley brimming with water.
2. In the midst of the valley stood a tree, whose color resembled that of fragrant trees, much like the mastic.
3. Along the valley's edges, I saw cinnamon trees emitting a rich fragrance, and beyond them, I continued my journey eastward.

Chapter 31

1. I came across another mountain range, where groves of trees flourished, exuding fragrant nectar known as Sarara and Galbanum.
2. Beyond these mountains, at the farthest reaches of the eastern lands, I encountered another mountain densely covered with aloe trees, their branches filled with stacte, resembling almond trees.
3. When burned, these trees released a fragrance sweeter than any other scent I had known.

Chapter 32

1. After encountering these rich fragrances, I turned my gaze northward over the mountains and saw seven peaks covered in choice nard, fragrant trees, cinnamon, and pepper.
2. I then traveled across the peaks of these mountains far to the east, passing over the Erythraean Sea and continuing beyond it, traversing above the domain of the angel Zotiel.
3. Eventually, I arrived at the Garden of Righteousness. From a distance, I saw trees more abundant and magnificent than any I had ever encountered. Among them, two trees stood out—remarkable in their beauty, splendor, and majesty. One was the Tree of Knowledge, whose sacred fruit grants profound wisdom.
4. This tree stood as tall as a fir, with leaves resembling those of a carob tree. Its fruit clustered like grapes on a vine, exuding extraordinary beauty. The fragrance of this tree extended far and wide.
5. I marveled, saying, "This tree is stunning—how wonderful it is to look upon!"

6. Then Raphael, the holy angel accompanying me, explained, "This is the Tree of Wisdom. Your ancestors, in their later years, ate from it. Upon consuming its fruit, their understanding was awakened—they gained wisdom, perceived their nakedness, and as a result, were expelled from the garden."

Chapter 33

1. From that place, I continued my journey to the farthest reaches of the earth, where I beheld enormous creatures, each distinct from the other, as well as birds of various kinds, differing in appearance, beauty, and sound, each unique in its own way.
2. To the east of these creatures, I reached the boundary of the earth, where the heavens rest upon it and where the gates of the heavens open.
3. I observed the emergence of the stars from these celestial portals, carefully counting each opening through which they appeared. I documented their movements, noting their numbers, names, paths, locations, seasons, and cycles, as revealed to me by Uriel, the holy angel who accompanied me.

4. He disclosed all this knowledge, instructing me to write down the names, laws, and divisions of the stars.

Chapter 34

1. Then, I journeyed north to the ends of the earth, where I encountered a magnificent and extraordinary formation at the boundary of the land. There, I saw three heavenly portals open in the sky, allowing the winds from the north to pass through, bringing cold, hail, frost, snow, dew, and rain.
2. One of these portals released winds that were favorable, while the other two let forth gales of great force, bringing hardship upon the earth, as they roared with tremendous power.

Chapter 35

1. From there, I traveled westward to the edge of the earth, where I observed three heavenly portals opening, just as I had seen in the east. They were identical in number and function, serving as outlets for the winds of heaven.

Chapter 36

1. Then, I journeyed to the southernmost part of the earth, where I observed three portals open in the heavens.
2. Through these openings, the winds, rain, and dew descended upon the earth. From there, I turned back toward the east, reaching the boundary of the heavens, where I saw three more portals open in the east, with smaller ones positioned above them.
3. These smaller portals served as passages for the stars of heaven as they moved westward, following the paths appointed to them. Each time I beheld these wonders, I gave praise to the Lord of Glory, continually exalting Him for His magnificent and awe-inspiring works. He has revealed the grandeur of His creation to the angels, spirits, and humankind so that all may witness His might, admire the wonders of His craftsmanship, and offer Him praise for eternity.

The Book of Parables - Enoch's Ethiopic Book 2

Chapter 37

1. This is the second vision of wisdom that came to Enoch, the son of Jared, the son of

Mahalalel, the son of Cainan, the son of Enos, the son of Seth, the son of Adam.

2. These are the words of wisdom that I lifted my voice to declare to those on earth: "Hear me, you who lived in ancient times, and you who will come after, for I will speak before the Lord of Spirits."
3. This wisdom might have been reserved for those of old, but it is not withheld from those who are yet to come.
4. Until now, such understanding has not been granted by the Lord of Spirits as it has now been revealed to me, according to His will. He has granted me the gift of eternal life.
5. I was given three parables, and I raised my voice to share them with those who dwell on the earth.

Chapter 38

1. The First Parable: When the gathering of the righteous takes place, sinners will be judged for their deeds and cast away from the face of the earth.

2. When the Righteous One is revealed before the just, those whose works are upheld by the Lord of Spirits, light will shine upon the righteous and the chosen who dwell on the earth. But where will the sinners find a place? Where will those who rejected the Lord of Spirits go? It would have been better for them never to have been born.
3. When the mysteries of the righteous are made known and the judgment is passed upon sinners, the wicked will be banished from the presence of the holy and the chosen.
4. From that moment on, the powerful and the mighty who rule the earth will no longer be exalted. They will not be able to look upon the holy, for the Lord of Spirits will shine His light upon the faces of the righteous, the just, and the chosen.
5. Then, the rulers and the strong ones will perish, handed over into the authority of the holy and the righteous.
6. At that time, no one will seek mercy from the Lord of Spirits, for their days will have come to an end.

Chapter 39

1. In those days, the chosen and the holy ones will descend from the heavens.
2. Their offspring will join with the children of men. During that time, Enoch received writings of wrath and judgment, along with records of banishment and exile, and the Lord of Spirits declared that mercy would not be granted to them.
3. In those days, I was lifted by a whirlwind from the earth and taken to the ends of the heavens.
4. There, I saw another vision—dwelling places prepared for the holy and resting places for the righteous.
5. My eyes beheld their homes among the righteous angels, their resting places among the holy. They lifted prayers, intercessions, and supplications for humanity, and righteousness flowed before them like water, while mercy descended like dew upon the earth. This will be their state for eternity.
6. In that place, I saw the Chosen One of righteousness and faith, dwelling beneath the wings of the Lord of Spirits. Righteousness will flourish in His time, and the righteous and chosen will be without number before Him forever.

7. All the righteous and chosen will shine like fiery lights before Him, their mouths filled with blessings, and their lips declaring praises to the name of the Lord of Spirits. Righteousness will never cease before Him, and truth will never falter.
8. My spirit longed to remain there, for my heart desired that place. This was my destined portion, decreed for me by the Lord of Spirits.
9. In those days, I praised and exalted the name of the Lord of Spirits with blessings and hymns, for He had appointed me for blessings and honor according to His will.
10. My eyes remained fixed on that place for a long time, and I continued blessing and praising, saying: "Blessed is He, and may He be praised from the beginning and forevermore." He exists without end; He knew all things before creation and understands everything across generations.
11. Those who do not sleep bless Him continuously; they stand before His glory, praising Him, saying, "Holy, holy, holy is the Lord of Spirits, who fills the earth with spirits."
12. I saw all those who do not sleep, standing before Him in praise, declaring, "Blessed are

You, and blessed is Your name, O Lord, forever and ever."

Chapter 40

1. After this, I witnessed an immense assembly—countless thousands upon thousands, an unending multitude—standing before the Lord of Spirits.
2. Among them, I saw four distinct figures who approached the presence of the Lord of Spirits. Their appearance was unlike any other, for they neither rested nor slept but stood continuously in His presence, offering unceasing praise.
3. I heard their voices as they lifted their praises before the Lord of Glory.
4. The first voice proclaimed blessings upon the Lord of Spirits, exalting Him for all eternity.
5. The second voice blessed the Chosen One and those who put their trust in the Lord of Spirits.
6. The third voice offered praise to the holy ones and to the spirits of the righteous.
7. The fourth voice removed the presence of wicked spirits, preventing them from

standing before the Lord of Spirits and accusing the saints who dwell on earth.

8. I turned to the angel who was with me and asked, "Who are these four beings whose voices I have heard and whose praises I have recorded?"
9. He answered, "The first is Michael, known for his mercy and patience. The second, who watches over the afflictions and suffering of humanity, is Raphael. The third, who possesses great power over all things, is Gabriel. And the fourth, responsible for leading those who seek repentance and granting hope to those destined for eternal life, is Phanuel."
10. These are the four angels of the Lord of Spirits, and these are the voices I heard in my vision.

Chapter 41

1. After this, I was shown the hidden mysteries of the heavens—the order in which the kingdom is divided and how the deeds of humankind are weighed on the scales of judgment.

2. I saw the dwellings of the chosen and the holy ones, who are shielded under the care of the Lord of Spirits.
3. All the righteous and elect shone like brilliant lights, and their lips overflowed with praises as they exalted the name of the Lord of Spirits for all eternity.
4. I also witnessed the secrets of lightning and thunder—how they are separated and how they return to their designated places at the appointed times.
5. I observed the storehouses of the winds and how they are apportioned according to their purpose.
6. I saw where the rain and dew are kept, held back by the clouds that carry them across the earth.
7. I was shown the chambers of the sun and moon, their origins and destinations, and how one shines more brightly than the other.
8. Their rotations formed the perfect sequence of day and night, never faltering from their ordained course.
9. I beheld the wondrous arrangement of the stars, each set in place by divine command, called by name and fulfilling its unique purpose.

Chapter 42

1. Wisdom sought a place to dwell but found nowhere to rest. Though she longed for a home, she found no sanctuary.
2. So she returned to her origin, taking refuge among the angels of heaven.
3. Meanwhile, iniquity arose, searching for a place to establish itself among the children of men. It took root upon the earth, spreading wrongdoing in its wake.

Chapter 43

1. I saw another wonder among the stars of heaven, where each was called by name.
2. I observed the movements of light as they traveled across the heavens. I measured their paths and calculated the harmony of their cycles.
3. Their rotations produced dazzling flames, each unique in its radiance, with one surpassing the others in brightness.

Chapter 44

1. Again, I witnessed another remarkable sight regarding the stars: they blazed like fire, yet

they never strayed from their appointed courses.

Chapter 45

1. This is the second parable, revealing the fate of those who reject the name of the Lord of Spirits. They will have no place in heaven, nor shall they remain upon the earth.
2. This is the destiny of sinners who deny the name of the Lord of Spirits: they are preserved for a day of judgment and suffering.
3. On that day, the Chosen One will take His seat upon the throne of glory, and all His deeds will be revealed. The scales of justice will measure the works of sinners, and their actions will be judged.
4. Heaven and earth will rejoice, and the chosen ones of heaven will dwell among them.
5. On that day, the Chosen One will live among the righteous, and the elect will walk at His side. All will witness His majesty.
6. Wickedness will vanish from the earth, and righteousness will flourish. The righteous will inherit eternal life, and the Lord of Spirits will dwell among them forever.

Chapter 46

1. I beheld the Chosen One seated upon a throne of glory, resembling a man but radiating divine majesty and splendor.
2. All the kings, rulers, and powerful of the earth stood before Him, bowing their faces in reverence.
3. Trembling seized them, and they were filled with such fear that they could not lift their eyes to look upon Him.
4. The mighty ones of the earth tried to speak, but their voices failed them. Their thoughts were scattered, and they were overcome with terror.
5. I saw the angels of judgment preparing chains and instruments of justice for the rulers and leaders of the world.
6. They will be handed over to the righteous and the chosen, no longer able to exalt themselves above them, for their time of judgment will come swiftly, and they will be cast down from their power.
7. The Chosen One will judge them in truth and righteousness, for He is the one appointed to rule over all.

Chapter 47

1. In those days, the prayers of the righteous and the cries of the just will ascend before the Lord of Spirits.
2. The holy ones in heaven will unite in one voice, offering praises and thanksgiving to the Lord of Spirits on behalf of those who have suffered on earth. They will intercede for the righteous, remembering the innocent blood that has been shed, and they will plead for justice.
3. The Most Holy One will hear their prayers and respond with righteous judgment. The days of the wicked will be brought to an end, and oppression will cease.
4. The earth will be cleansed of all wrongdoing, and the unjust will be removed from its midst. The righteous will dwell in peace, and their prayers will no longer go unanswered.

Chapter 48

1. In that place, I saw a wellspring of righteousness that flowed without end, surrounded by fountains of wisdom. All who

thirsted came to drink and were filled with knowledge.
2. At that moment, the Son of Man was named before the Lord of Spirits,
3. Before the stars were formed and before the foundations of the earth were set in place.
4. He was chosen to be the light for the righteous, to reign over them and give them strength and hope.
5. Through His name, salvation will come, and all the nations of the earth will bow before Him in reverence.
6. He will be a guiding light to the peoples, and His presence will bring everlasting peace.
7. The rulers and powerful of the earth will fall before Him, for none will be able to stand against His authority.
8. He will grant wisdom and righteousness to the chosen, and they will rejoice in His presence forever.
9. The righteous and the elect will be saved by His name, and their inheritance will be eternal life.

Chapter 49

1. The Lord of Spirits has poured out wisdom abundantly upon the righteous, leaving nothing hidden from them.
2. Wisdom becomes their guiding light and the source of their honor.
3. The chosen and the righteous are filled with divine wisdom, enabling them to dwell in peace forever. The power of the Lord of Spirits will remain with them, and they will be in the presence of the Son of Man, abiding in everlasting righteousness and glory.
4. The Lord of Spirits will impart the spirit of wisdom to His elect, allowing them to live in perpetual righteousness and tranquility.

Chapter 50

1. In those days, the righteous and the chosen will undergo a transformation. They will be surrounded by an unending light, and glory will be bestowed upon the holy ones.
2. This will occur on the day of great tribulation, when the accumulated wickedness is unleashed upon sinners. The righteous will stand victorious through the name of the Lord of Spirits. The wicked will witness the

triumph of the righteous, given a final chance to turn from their ways.
3. However, they will not receive honor through the name of the Lord of Spirits. Even so, they may still find salvation through His mercy, for the Lord of Spirits is compassionate.
4. Yet, His judgments remain just, and iniquity cannot stand in His presence. Those who refuse to repent will be removed from before Him.
5. From that day forward, the Lord of Spirits declares that mercy will no longer be extended to those who persist in their sins.

Chapter 51

1. In those days, the earth will return all that has been entrusted to it. The underworld will release what it holds, and Sheol will give up its captives.
2. For in that time, the Elect One will rise, choosing the righteous and the holy for the day of their deliverance is near.
3. The Elect One will take His seat upon God's throne, and from His lips will pour forth the wisdom and counsel bestowed upon Him by the Lord of Spirits, who has glorified Him.

4. In those days, the mountains will leap like rams, and the hills will rejoice like lambs, filled with gladness.
5. The heavens will shine with the joy of the angels, the earth will exult, and the righteous will dwell securely, walking in peace upon the land prepared for them.

Chapter 52

1. After those events, I was taken to the place where I had previously seen hidden mysteries in my visions. A powerful wind carried me toward the west.
2. There, I beheld mountains of iron, copper, silver, gold, molten metal, and lead.
3. I turned to the angel accompanying me and asked, "What are these things that have been revealed to me in secret?"
4. He replied, "These materials exist to serve the dominion of the Anointed One, granting Him strength upon the earth."
5. Then the angel of peace said, "Be patient, for soon all hidden things surrounding the Lord of Spirits will be made known to you."
6. He continued, "These mountains of iron, copper, silver, gold, molten metal, and lead

will all melt before the Elect One, dissolving like wax before fire or flowing like water. They will be powerless in His presence."
7. In those days, wealth will be of no use—neither gold nor silver will deliver anyone, and none will escape judgment.
8. Iron will no longer be fashioned into weapons, and armor will lose its value. Bronze will no longer be sought for war, tin will serve no purpose, and lead will be disregarded.
9. All these things will vanish from the earth when the Elect One appears before the Lord of Spirits.

Chapter 53

1. I saw a vast valley with open mouths, awaiting the offerings of all who dwell on the earth, sea, and islands. Though they bring gifts in reverence, the valley will never be filled.
2. The hands of sinners commit injustices, devouring those they oppress. Yet, they will be wiped away from the presence of the Lord of Spirits and removed from His creation, perishing forever.

3. I observed angels of punishment stationed there, preparing instruments of destruction for Satan.
4. I turned to the angel of peace and asked, "For whom are these weapons being prepared?"
5. He responded, "These are meant for the kings and rulers of the earth, who will meet their destruction by them."
6. After this, the Righteous and Elect One will establish the dwelling place for His people, and from that time, they will no longer be troubled in the name of the Lord of Spirits.
7. The great mountains will crumble and flow like rivers, and the righteous will find peace, free from the oppression of sinners.

Chapter 54

1. I turned and looked at another part of the earth and saw a deep valley filled with consuming fire.
2. The kings and rulers were brought there and thrown into the valley.
3. I saw that they were bound with heavy chains of iron that could not be broken.
4. I asked the angel of peace, "For whom are these chains prepared?"

5. He answered, "These chains are meant for the army of Azazel, to bind them and cast them into the abyss of eternal condemnation. The Lord of Spirits has decreed that rough stones will seal their mouths."
6. On that great day, Michael, Gabriel, Raphael, and Phanuel will seize them and throw them into the blazing fire, where they will face judgment from the Lord of Spirits for their sins. They aligned themselves with Satan and led mankind astray.
7. In those days, divine judgment will be executed, and the waters above the heavens and the fountains of the deep will be opened.
8. The waters from above and below will merge—the upper waters from the heavens and the lower waters from the earth.
9. These floods will overwhelm the inhabitants of the earth, consuming all who dwell under the heavens.
10. When the sinners realize the consequences of their actions, they will perish in the flood.

Chapter 55

1. Then the Ancient of Days reflected, saying, "In vain have I destroyed all the inhabitants of the earth."
2. He swore by His great name, "Never again will I bring such destruction upon the earth. As long as the heavens exist above the earth, I will set a sign as a covenant between Me and mankind, a lasting testimony."
3. However, when I call upon them for judgment during a time of tribulation and affliction, My punishment and wrath will remain upon them, declares the Lord of Spirits.
4. "You mighty kings who dwell upon the earth will see My Chosen One. He will sit upon His throne of glory and execute judgment upon Azazel, his followers, and all who stand with him, in the name of the Lord of Spirits."

Chapter 56

1. I saw a host of angels carrying scourges and chains of iron and bronze, marching forward.
2. I asked the angel of peace, "Where are they going with these instruments?"

3. He replied, "They are on their way to seize those who are marked for judgment and cast them into the abyss of the valley."
4. That valley will be filled with their chosen and beloved ones, and their days of leading others astray will come to an end.
5. In those times, the angels will descend upon the Parthians and Medes, stirring up their kings and filling them with unrest. They will rise from their thrones, charging forth like lions from their dens and like ravenous wolves among their prey.
6. They will trample upon the land of the Elect, turning it into a battlefield and a wasteland.
7. Yet, the city of the righteous will resist them. Strife will break out among them, brother will turn against brother, and father against son. Their slaughter will leave countless dead, and their punishment will not be in vain.
8. Sheol will open its gates, swallowing them whole, ensuring their complete destruction. Sinners will be consumed in the presence of the Elect.

Chapter 57

1. After this, I saw a great number of chariots and riders coming from the east, west, and south, carried by the winds.
2. The sound of their chariots roared through the heavens, shaking the very foundations of the earth, and the holy ones above marveled at the spectacle. The pillars of the world trembled as the noise echoed across the heavens in a single day.
3. All shall fall down and worship the Lord of Spirits. Thus concludes the second parable.

Chapter 58

1. I began to proclaim the third parable concerning the righteous and the elect.
2. "Blessed are you, O righteous and elect, for your inheritance will be filled with glory.
3. The righteous will dwell in the light of the sun, and the elect in the radiance of eternal life. Their days will be unending, and the lives of the holy will be without limit.
4. They will seek the light and find righteousness with the Lord of Spirits, and peace shall be theirs forever in His name.
5. It will be declared in heaven that the mysteries of righteousness should be

revealed to the holy and faithful, shining like the sun upon the earth as darkness is forever removed.

6. A light will be established that never fades, and days that know no end will come, for darkness will be destroyed, and righteousness will be eternally established before the Lord of Spirits."

Chapter 59

1. In those days, I witnessed the mysteries of the lightning and the lights, and how they are directed by divine command. They are sent forth for blessing or for judgment as the Lord of Spirits decrees.
2. I saw the secrets of thunder and the mighty sound that comes from above. The Lord allowed me to see the judgments that are carried out upon the earth—whether for goodness and blessing or for punishment—according to His word.
3. I was shown all the mysteries of light and the brilliance of the lightning, which shine forth as a sign of divine favor and fulfillment.

The Book Of Noah – Apocryphal Part Of Noah's Book Excluded From Canonical Bible

Chapter 60

1. In the five hundredth year, on the fourteenth day of the seventh month of Enoch's life, I was shown a vision. A great trembling shook the heavens, and the entire heavenly host, thousands upon thousands of angels, were deeply unsettled.
2. The Ancient of Days sat on His glorious throne, and the angels and the righteous stood around Him.
3. I was overcome with fear and trembling, feeling my strength leave me, and I fell to the ground.
4. Michael, an angel among the holy ones, sent another to raise me. When he lifted me up, my spirit returned to me, as I had not been able to endure the sight of that mighty host and the trembling heavens.

5. Michael asked me, "Why are you disturbed by this vision? Until now, the Lord has shown patience and mercy to those on earth.
6. But the day is coming, when the Lord's power, judgment, and wrath will fall upon those who ignore the righteous law, those who reject His judgment, and those who defile His name. That day is prepared: it will bring a covenant for the righteous and an inquisition for sinners.
7. On that day, two great beasts will be separated: Leviathan, the female, will reside in the abyss of the sea, over the fountains of the waters,
8. And Behemoth, the male, will live in a barren wilderness called Duidain, east of the garden where the elect and righteous dwell, where my forefather, the seventh from Adam, was taken up.
9. I asked the angel to show me the might of these creatures and how they were divided in one day, with one cast into the sea and the other into the wilderness.
10. The angel replied, "You, son of man, are seeking to understand mysteries that are hidden from you."

11. The other angel revealed to me the secrets of the heavens above, the depths of the earth below, and the boundary of the heavens and their foundations.
12. He showed me the storehouses of the winds, how they are separated, weighed, and measured according to their strength.
13. He also showed me the light of the moon, guided by angels, and revealed how the stars and lights obey the Lord.
14. Thunder has specific resting places where it waits to make its sound. Thunder and lightning move together, yet remain distinct; they follow each other in harmony and do not part.
15. When lightning flashes, thunder immediately follows, and their sounds are divided equally, controlled by the spirit and directed across the earth.
16. The spirit of the sea is powerful, bound by a rein, and then released to spread its waters among the mountains.
17. The spirit of frost has its own angel, and the spirit of hail is under the care of a righteous angel.

18. The spirit of snow comes from its chambers with great force, resembling smoke, and is known as frost.
19. The spirit of mist has its own domain and moves in both light and darkness, summer and winter, under the guidance of an angel.
20. The spirit of dew resides at the ends of the heavens, connected to the rain chambers, and its course continues through both winter and summer.
21. When the spirit of rain departs from its chamber, angels open it and guide it across the earth, where it unites with the waters below to nourish all life.
22. The waters provided by the Most High sustain the earth. The rain is measured, and the angels distribute it. I saw all of this near the Garden of the Righteous.
23. The angel of peace said to me, "These two creatures, created by God's greatness, will be preserved."

Chapter 61

1. In those days, I saw angels given long cords, and they flew to the north.

2. I asked the angel, "Why are these angels flying with cords?" He replied, "They are going to measure."
3. "These angels will measure the righteous and give them the cords of the righteous so they may rest on the name of the Lord of Spirits forever."
4. The elect will dwell with the elect, and the measures will strengthen righteousness.
5. These measures will reveal the earth's mysteries—those lost in deserts, devoured by beasts, or taken by the sea—so they may be restored on the day of the Elect One. None will perish before the Lord of Spirits.
6. All those who dwell in heaven received a command and power, and together, they blessed the Lord with one voice, their praise shining with fiery light.
7. With their first words, they extolled the Lord with wisdom, wise in word and spirit.
8. The Lord of Spirits placed the Elect One upon His throne of glory, where He will judge the deeds of the holy ones, balancing their actions.

Chapter 62

1. The Lord of Spirits commanded the kings, the mighty, the exalted, and all on earth, saying, "Open your eyes and lift your heads to recognize the Elect One."
2. The Lord seated Him on His throne of glory, and the spirit of righteousness was poured upon Him.
3. By His word, sinners will be slain, and the unrighteous will be destroyed from His presence.
4. On that day, all the kings, mighty ones, and rulers of the earth will see and recognize His glory, as He sits in judgment, and no false word will be spoken before Him.
5. They will be filled with fear, like a woman in labor, feeling the pain of childbirth.
6. They will look at each other in terror, filled with anguish when they see the Son of Man on His throne of glory. The kings and mighty ones will bless, glorify, and exalt Him, who rules over all and was once hidden.
7. From the beginning, the Son of Man was hidden, preserved by the Most High, and revealed to the elect.
8. On that day, the elect and holy will stand before Him.

9. All kings, rulers, and the mighty of the earth will fall before Him, worshiping and placing their hopes in the Son of Man, seeking mercy.
10. But the Lord of Spirits will turn them away, their faces filled with shame, as darkness deepens upon them.
11. He will deliver them to the angels for punishment, as retribution for the oppression of His children and the chosen.
12. They will become a spectacle to the righteous and elect, who will rejoice in the judgment of the Lord of Spirits upon them.
13. On that day, the righteous and elect will be saved, never again to see the face of sinners.
14. The Lord of Spirits will dwell among the righteous, and together with the Son of Man, they will eat, rest, and rise forever.
15. The righteous, having risen from the earth, will no longer be downcast, clothed in garments of glory.
16. These are garments of life, provided by the Lord of Spirits, which will never age or fade, enduring forever before the Lord.

Chapter 63

1. During that time, the rulers and the powerful of the earth will plead for mercy, seeking a brief respite from the angels of punishment to whom they have been delivered. They will beg for the chance to bow down and acknowledge the Lord of Spirits, confessing their wrongdoing.
2. They will glorify Him, saying, "Blessed is the Lord of Spirits, the Sovereign of kings, the Ruler of the mighty, the Master of the wealthy, the Source of glory, and the Fountain of wisdom."
3. "Your power is beyond comprehension, enduring from generation to generation. Your glory is everlasting, and Your ways are beyond measure."
4. "At last, we understand that we should have honored and praised the Lord of Spirits, the true King above all kings."
5. They will lament, "If only we had the chance to rest and give thanks, to declare our faith before His glory!"
6. "But now, we seek relief and find none. We search for light, but darkness is our eternal dwelling."
7. "We failed to believe in Him, to honor His name, or to recognize His authority. Instead,

we placed our trust in our kingdoms and our own power."
8. "Now, in our suffering, He does not come to save us, and our cries for help bring no relief. His judgments are just, and His ways are beyond dispute."
9. "We have been cast away because of our actions, and every sin we committed has been counted against us with righteousness."
10. In despair, they will admit, "We gathered wealth unjustly, but it does not save us from our descent into Sheol."
11. Their faces will be covered in shame before the Son of Man, and they will be driven from His presence, with the sword of judgment set before them.
12. Thus declares the Lord of Spirits: "This is the decree and the judgment for the rulers, the mighty, the exalted, and all who hold dominion on the earth."

Chapter 64

1. In that place, I saw other forms hidden away.
2. I heard the voice of an angel declare, "These are the angels who descended to the earth,

revealing forbidden knowledge to humankind, leading them into sin."

Chapter 65

1. In those days, Noah observed that the earth was collapsing and that its destruction was imminent.
2. Distressed, he traveled to the ends of the earth, crying out to his grandfather, Enoch, with a sorrowful plea: "Hear me, hear me, hear me!"
3. I responded to him, "Tell me what is happening to the earth, why it is trembling and in such turmoil, so that I may not perish with it."
4. Suddenly, a great disturbance shook the land, and a voice from heaven was heard, causing me to fall upon my face.
5. Then my grandfather, Enoch, stood beside me, saying, "Why do you cry out with such anguish?"
6. "A command has been given from the Lord concerning those who dwell on the earth. Their fate has been sealed because they have sought the hidden knowledge of the angels,

the dark arts of the Satans, and the secret powers of the fallen ones."
7. "They have embraced sorcery, witchcraft, and the creation of molten images, corrupting the entire world. They have also learned how silver is drawn from the earth, how soft metals are extracted, and the mysteries of their origins."
8. "For lead and tin do not emerge like other metals; they come from a secret source, and an angel oversees their flow."
9. Then my grandfather, Enoch, took my hand and lifted me up, saying, "Come, for I have sought the Lord of Spirits regarding this great disturbance upon the earth."
10. He answered, 'Their judgment has been set, and I will no longer delay it. Because of their corruption and the knowledge they have stolen, the entire earth and its inhabitants will be destroyed.'"
11. "There is no repentance for them, for they have exposed what was forbidden. Their condemnation is final. But you, my son, are known to the Lord of Spirits, and you are free from this transgression."
12. "He has chosen you to stand among the holy ones, to be preserved among those who will

remain. From your lineage, rulers will arise, and great honor will be given to your descendants. From you, a fountain of righteousness will spring forth, without end."

Chapter 66

1. After this, I was shown the angels of judgment, prepared to unleash the mighty forces of the waters beneath the earth to bring destruction upon its inhabitants.
2. The Lord of Spirits commanded the angels to restrain the waters, holding them back, for these angels have dominion over the deep.
3. Then I departed from the presence of Enoch.

Chapter 67

1. In those days, the word of the Lord came to me, saying, "Noah, you have been chosen before Me as righteous, upright, and full of love."
2. "Now, the angels are constructing a wooden vessel, and when their work is complete, I will lay My hand upon it to preserve it. From

this, life will be sustained, and the earth will not remain desolate."
3. "Your descendants will be established before Me forever, and those who are with you shall prosper. They will not be barren but will multiply and be blessed in My name."
4. "The angels who have acted wickedly will be confined in a fiery valley, the same one my grandfather Enoch showed me in the west, among mountains of gold, silver, iron, lead, and tin."
5. I saw that valley, and a great disturbance of water erupted within it.
6. As this occurred, molten metals mixed with the waters, producing a strong sulfurous smell. Beneath this land burned the valley of those angels who led humanity astray.
7. Fiery streams flowed through its depths, where those fallen angels were being punished.
8. In the days to come, these waters will be used by the kings, the mighty, and the rulers of the earth. They will cleanse the body but bring torment to the spirit, for they denied the Lord and followed their own desires.

9. As their physical suffering increases, their spirits will be changed forever, for no one can stand in defiance before the Lord.
10. They will be judged for indulging in the desires of the flesh while rejecting the Spirit of the Lord.
11. In those days, these judgmental waters will shift—when the angels are punished within them, the springs will change their temperature. As they ascend, the waters will turn cold.
12. Then I heard Michael declare, "This judgment upon the angels serves as a testimony against the rulers and the mighty of the earth."
13. "These waters will provide healing for their bodies and satisfy their cravings, yet they fail to understand that these same waters will one day transform into an eternal fire."

Chapter 68

1. After this, my grandfather Enoch revealed to me all the mysteries found in the Book of Parables, which had been given to him. He carefully arranged these teachings and compiled them for me.

2. On that day, Michael spoke to Raphael, saying, "The power of the spirit fills me with dread because of the severity of this judgment—its finality, its hidden decrees, and the fate of the fallen angels. Who can withstand such a terrible verdict?"

3. Again, Michael spoke, "Is there anyone among us whose heart is not troubled by this judgment upon them? Who does not feel the weight of their fate, knowing they led others astray?"

4. As he stood before the Lord of Spirits, Michael said to Raphael, "I will not intercede for them, for they have defied the Lord of Spirits and sought to exalt themselves as if they were gods."

5. "For this reason, all hidden things will be revealed against them, and they alone will bear the weight of their punishment for eternity—no angel or human will share in it."

Chapter 69

1. After this judgment was passed, fear and trembling overtook them, for they had revealed the secrets of heaven to humanity.

2. Here are the names of the fallen angels: the first is Samjaza, the second is Artaqifa, the third is Armen, the fourth is Kokabel, the fifth is Turael, the sixth is Rumjal, the seventh is Danjal, the eighth is Neqael, the ninth is Baraqel, the tenth is Azazel, the eleventh is Armaros, the twelfth is Batarjal, the thirteenth is Busasejal, the fourteenth is Hananel, the fifteenth is Turel, the sixteenth is Simapesiel, the seventeenth is Jetrel, the eighteenth is Tumael, the nineteenth is Turel, and the twentieth is Rumael.
3. These were the leaders among them, each commanding groups of hundreds, fifties, and tens.
4. The first, Jeqon, misled the holy ones, drawing them down to the earth through their desire for the daughters of men.
5. The second, Asbeel, deceived the sons of God with wicked counsel, leading them into corruption.
6. The third, Gadreel, introduced death to humanity, deceived Eve, and taught mankind the art of warfare—shields, armor, and the weapons of battle.
7. From his hand, instruments of death were spread throughout the earth.

8. The fourth, Penemue, revealed the knowledge of good and evil, teaching the secrets of wisdom.
9. He introduced writing with ink and parchment, leading many to sin through the knowledge he shared.
10. Humanity was not created for such purposes, to establish their faith through writing.
11. They were meant to be like the angels, pure and righteous, never subject to death. Yet through this knowledge, they fell, and it grieves me deeply.
12. The fifth, Kasdeja, revealed the workings of spirits and demons, the strikes upon the unborn in the womb, and the wounds that afflict the soul. He also taught about serpent bites and the scorching effects of the noonday sun.
13. Kasbeel, the chief of the oath, disclosed this to the holy ones in his glory, and his name is Biqa.
14. This angel sought the hidden name from Michael, desiring to wield its power and cause those who revealed divine secrets to tremble.
15. The power of this oath is great; Michael sealed it in his hand, calling it Akae.

16. By this oath, the heavens were upheld before the world was formed, and they will remain for eternity.
17. Through this oath, the earth was anchored upon the waters, and the deep waters of the mountains flow forth unceasingly.
18. The sea was set in place by this oath, and the sand was given as its boundary, preventing it from overflowing.
19. The abyss was secured by this oath, unmoving from generation to generation.
20. By it, the sun and moon follow their paths, never deviating from their ordained courses.
21. By it, the stars shine in their appointed places, answering when He calls them.
22. Likewise, the spirits of the winds and waters, along with all the elements, abide by their assigned duties.
23. The thunders, lightnings, and storehouses of hail, frost, mist, rain, and dew are governed by this oath.
24. These forces offer unceasing praise to the Lord of Spirits, exalting His name above all else.
25. This oath holds them in place, preserving the order of creation.

26. They rejoiced greatly when the name of the Son of Man was revealed to them.
27. He took His seat upon the throne of glory, and judgment was entrusted to Him. He decreed the downfall of sinners and removed those who led the world astray.
28. They were bound in chains and cast into the place of their destruction, their works erased from the earth.
29. From that moment on, nothing corruptible will endure, for the Son of Man reigns on His throne, and all wickedness is banished from His sight. His word stands firm before the Lord of Spirits.

Chapter 70

1. After these events, during Enoch's lifetime, his name was exalted among the living as the Son of Man, known before the Lord of Spirits.
2. Enoch was taken up in the chariots of the spirit, disappearing from among men. From that day forward, he was no longer counted among them, for he was placed between the North and the West.

3. There, the angels measured the place reserved for the righteous and the elect.
4. I beheld the ancient fathers and the holy ones who had lived from the beginning.

Chapter 71

1. After these events, my spirit was carried away into the heavens, where I beheld the holy sons of God moving upon flames of fire. Their garments gleamed white, and their faces shone with a brilliance like snow.
2. I saw two rivers of fire flowing, their light glowing like hyacinth, and I fell upon my face before the Lord of Spirits.
3. Then Michael, one of the archangels, took my right hand, lifted me up, and guided me through the hidden truths, revealing the mysteries of righteousness.
4. He showed me the farthest reaches of the heavens, the chambers where the stars reside, and the paths of the celestial bodies that journey before the holy ones.
5. My spirit ascended to the highest heaven, where I saw a structure formed of crystals, interwoven with streams of living fire.

6. My spirit beheld the radiant girdle encircling that house of fire, and on each of its four sides, rivers of living fire flowed ceaselessly.
7. Surrounding it were Seraphim, Cherubim, and Ophanim—beings who never sleep but remain in constant vigil over the throne of His glory.
8. I saw multitudes of angels, countless in number, encircling that house—thousands upon thousands and ten thousand times ten thousand.
9. Michael, Raphael, Gabriel, Phanuel, and the other holy angels who dwell above entered and departed from that place.
10. Then the Ancient of Days emerged, His head white as wool, His garments indescribably radiant.
11. I fell to my face, overcome with weakness, and my spirit was transformed. I cried out in praise, blessing and glorifying the Lord of Spirits.
12. The words of my blessing were well received by the Ancient of Days, who stood with Michael, Gabriel, Raphael, Phanuel, and an innumerable host of angels.
13. In this vision, a portion was lost, but it described the presence of the Son of Man

alongside the Ancient of Days. Enoch inquired about the identity of this Son of Man.

14. The angel turned to me and said, "This is the Son of Man, the one in whom righteousness dwells, and righteousness shall never depart from Him."
15. "He is the bringer of peace in the name of the world to come, for peace has existed with Him from the beginning and shall endure forever."
16. "All shall follow His ways, for righteousness shall never depart from Him. With Him shall be the dwelling and the inheritance of the righteous, and they shall never be separated from Him."
17. "Eternal life shall be with the Son of Man, and the righteous will abide in peace, walking uprightly before the Lord of Spirits forever."

The Book of the Luminaries of the Heaven – Enoch's Ethiopic Book 3

Chapter 72

1. This is the record of the movements of the heavenly luminaries, describing their paths according to their classifications, times, seasons, and assigned names, as well as their places of origin and the months in which they move. Uriel, the holy angel who guides them, revealed their order to me, showing me their precise laws governing the years of the world and the eternal cycles, leading to the renewal of all creation.
2. The first law of the luminaries concerns the great light, the sun, which rises through the portals of the east and sets in the western gates of the heavens.
3. I observed six portals from which the sun ascends and six from which it descends, and through these same portals, the moon and stars also follow their courses in perfect order.
4. In addition to these portals, I saw many small windows positioned on either side of them.
5. The first and greatest luminary, the sun, has a circumference like that of heaven and is filled with a brilliant and consuming fire.
6. It ascends in a chariot that is carried by the wind. Descending from the heavens, it travels through the northern regions to return to the

eastern portals, from which it shines upon the sky.
7. In the first month, the sun rises in the fourth portal of the eastern sky. There are twelve windows in this portal, from which flames emerge at their designated times.
8. As it rises from the fourth portal, it follows this path for thirty days, setting precisely in the fourth portal of the western sky.
9. During this period, the daylight grows longer while the night shortens, with the day surpassing the night by one-ninth. The day then becomes ten parts, and the night eight parts.
10. Following this, the sun rises in the fifth eastern portal for thirty more days.
11. The day further lengthens by two parts, reaching eleven, while the night diminishes to seven.
12. The sun then ascends through the sixth portal, following this path for thirty-one days, adhering to its sign.
13. At this time, the daylight doubles the length of the night, reaching twelve parts, while the night is reduced to six parts.

14. After this, the sun begins to shorten the day while extending the night, continuing in the sixth portal for another thirty days.
15. At the conclusion of this phase, the day decreases by one part, equaling eleven parts, while the night increases to seven parts.
16. Then the sun moves into the fifth portal for thirty days.
17. The day shortens again, reaching ten parts, while the night extends to eight parts.
18. The sun then follows the fourth portal for thirty-one days, and on that day, the length of day and night become equal, each having nine parts.
19. The sun then transitions to the third portal for thirty days, causing the night to overtake the day, reaching ten parts, while the day reduces to eight.
20. Moving to the second portal, it follows this course for thirty days.
21. The night increases further, reaching eleven parts, while the day diminishes to seven.
22. The sun then moves into the first portal for thirty-one days.
23. At this stage, the night doubles the length of the day, with twelve parts, while the day consists of six parts.

24. Completing its cycle, the sun returns to the first portal for another thirty days.
25. During this phase, the night decreases by one part, becoming eleven parts, while the day extends to seven.
26. The sun transitions to the second portal for thirty days.
27. The night continues to shorten, reaching ten parts, while the day increases to eight.
28. The sun follows the second portal again before moving into the third portal for thirty-one days.
29. At this point, the night decreases to nine parts, and the day grows to nine parts, marking the completion of a 364-day year.
30. The varying lengths of day and night are determined by the sun's movement throughout its cycle.
31. The sun governs the expansion of daylight and the shortening of night, and this pattern is consistent throughout its journey.
32. This is the law governing the sun's motion, as it completes its circuit sixty times, always rising and setting in its designated portals.
33. This great luminary, the sun, is named according to its function, as decreed by the Lord.

34. Although the sun and moon are equal in size, the sun's brightness is seven times greater than that of the moon. However, their cycles remain in harmony, as set by divine law.

Chapter 73

1. After observing the laws governing the sun, I turned my attention to another luminary, the moon, which follows its own unique cycle.
2. Its movement is guided by the wind, and it receives its light in measured portions. Its rising and setting vary each month.
3. The moon's cycle mirrors that of the sun, and when fully illuminated, it shines with one-seventh of the brightness of the sun.
4. On the thirtieth morning, the moon begins its new phase in the east, marking the start of its cycle as it rises in the same portal as the sun.
5. At this stage, only one-seventh of its light is visible, while the rest remains dark.
6. With each passing day, its light increases by one-seventh.
7. As the sun rises, the moon also rises, gradually gaining more of the sun's light.

8. It continues this process, increasing in illumination each night, until it reaches its full brightness after thirteen parts.

Chapter 74

1. I observed yet another law concerning the moon's motion and its monthly cycle.
2. Uriel, the holy angel, revealed its path to me, explaining how it progresses through its phases until the fifteenth day.
3. The moon reaches full brightness in the east before gradually darkening in the west, following a precise pattern of seventh divisions.
4. In some months, the moon alters its setting position, while in others, it follows a distinct path.
5. During two months of the year, the moon sets with the sun through the third and fourth eastern portals.
6. It advances for seven days, then turns back, entering the sixth portal, where it reaches full illumination as it moves away from the sun.
7. Afterward, it returns to the fourth portal, remaining there for seven days before gradually dimming.

8. The moon then retreats to the first portal, completing its cycle.
9. Its movements align with the sun's setting position, ensuring their orbits remain in harmony.
10. Every five years, an additional thirty days are added to complete the solar year of 364 days.
11. The extra days from the sun and the stars contribute six additional days annually, totaling thirty over five years.
12. The moon, lagging behind the sun and stars, accounts for this difference, ensuring the balance of time.
13. Over eight years, the moon falls behind by eighty days, completing its cycle alongside the sun and stars.

Chapter 75

1. The heavenly hosts, who oversee creation and the celestial bodies, also regulate the four intercalary days that are not counted within the standard year.
2. Many people misunderstand the correct positioning of these luminaries, which are fixed in the first, third, fourth, and sixth portals, completing the year with 364 days.

3. Uriel, the angel appointed by the Lord of Glory, governs these celestial bodies, revealing their signs, seasons, years, and appointed times.
4. He showed me twelve portals in the heavens, from which the sun's light emerges, spreading warmth over the earth.
5. These portals, located at the edges of the heavens, allow the sun, moon, and stars to pass through, dictating the cycles of the skies.
6. Numerous small windows flank each portal, releasing warmth at their designated times. Above these portals, I saw celestial chariots moving across the heavens, carrying the stars that never set. Among them, one larger chariot traversed the entire world.

Chapter 76

1. At the farthest ends of the earth, I observed twelve great portals through which the winds of heaven blow over the world.
2. Three portals are positioned toward the east, three toward the west, three toward the north, and three toward the south.
3. Each set of three governs the winds from its respective direction: the first three belong to

the east, followed by those of the north, the south, and finally, the west.
4. Four of these winds bring blessings and prosperity, while the remaining eight cause destruction upon the earth and its inhabitants.
5. The first portal of the east wind brings desolation, drought, intense heat, and ruin.
6. The second portal of the east wind brings rainfall, fruitfulness, prosperity, and dew.
7. The third eastern portal brings cold winds and dryness.
8. From an adjacent portal, fragrant scents emerge, filling the air.
9. The first portal of the southern winds carries intense heat, while the second portal brings prosperity, good health, and rain. The third portal brings both dew and destruction.
10. The northern winds bring cold and rain through the first portal, while the second portal provides healing, dew, and prosperity. The third northern portal delivers frost, snow, and plagues of locusts.
11. The western winds bring frost, dew, and rain through the first portal. The second portal grants prosperity and blessings, while the third portal causes drought and devastation.

12. These twelve portals regulate the winds and their effects on the earth, determining whether they bring blessings or calamities.

Chapter 77

1. The first direction, the east, is regarded as the principal quarter. The second, the south, is where the Most High will descend, a land uniquely chosen and blessed for His coming.
2. The west is referred to as the diminished quarter because all celestial bodies in the heavens fade and set there.
3. The northern region is divided into three sections: one designated for human habitation, another containing seas, abysses, rivers, forests, and clouds, and the last housing the garden of righteousness.
4. I saw seven towering mountains, the highest on earth, from which frost originates.
5. The measurement of time—days, seasons, and years—is determined from these mountains.
6. Additionally, I saw seven mighty rivers, greater than all others on earth. One flows westward into the Great Sea.

7. Two rivers originate in the north and flow eastward into the Erythraean Sea. The remaining four rivers flow toward different seas; two enter the Erythraean Sea, while the other two flow into the Great Sea, though some claim they end in the desert.
8. I also observed seven great islands, two on the mainland and five within the Great Sea.

Chapter 78

1. The sun is known by two names: the first is Orjares, and the second is Tomas.
2. The moon has four names: Asonja, Ebla, Benase, and Erae.
3. These two celestial bodies are of similar size, resembling the heavens in their circumference.
4. However, the sun's light surpasses the moon's by seven portions, and it transfers measured light to the moon until its own seventh portion is diminished.
5. Both the sun and moon complete their circuits, entering through the western portals, turning northward, and emerging again through the eastern portals to traverse the heavens.

6. As the moon begins its journey, one-fourteenth of it becomes visible.
7. It continues to gain light until, by the fourteenth day, it reaches its full radiance.
8. On the fifteenth day, the moon shines at its brightest before gradually diminishing. Each day, it loses one-fourteenth of its light
9. Until, by the fifteenth day, it disappears entirely.
10. Some months contain twenty-nine days, while others have twenty-eight.
11. Uriel, the holy angel, revealed another law: the sun bestows its light upon the moon, and during its waxing, the moon gathers light for fourteen days until fully illuminated.
12. The new moon becomes visible on the day it receives its initial light.
13. By the fifteenth day, it reaches full brightness, rising in opposition to the setting sun.
14. Throughout the night, the moon shines until the sun reappears, after which it begins to wane until all its light vanishes, marking the end of the month.
15. The moon follows a structured cycle, with three months consisting of thirty days and three months consisting of twenty-nine days.

16. This cycle is precise, allowing the moon to be visible for twenty days each month, shining at night and appearing like the heavens by day, though lacking the same radiance.

Chapter 79

1. "Now, my son, I have shown you all that has been revealed to me, and the laws of the stars are complete."
2. "I have been granted insight into every law that governs the stars, detailing their movements for each day, season, year, month, and week."
3. "The moon's waning occurs when it passes through the sixth portal, where its light diminishes
4. Until it fades entirely."
5. "It continues its journey through the portals, completing a cycle of 177 days, which equals twenty-five weeks and two days."
6. "In each cycle, the moon falls behind the sun by five days, in accordance with the instructions given by Uriel, the archangel overseeing the stars."

Chapter 80

1. "The angel Uriel said to me, 'Enoch, I have now shown you all things—the paths of the sun and moon, the leaders of the stars, their responsibilities, their appointed times, and their exits.'"
2. "'In the days of the wicked, the years will become shorter, and the land will fail to yield its produce as it once did.'"
3. "'All natural cycles will be disrupted—seasons will no longer be predictable, the rain will cease, and the sky will no longer send its waters upon the earth.'"
4. "'The crops of the earth will be delayed, growing out of their proper seasons, and the fruit of the trees will be withheld.'"
5. "'The moon will shift from its intended course, failing to appear as expected.'"
6. "'The sun will set in the west but will shine with an intensity beyond what is anticipated, altering the natural balance of light.'"
7. "'Many stars will stray from their designated paths, disrupting their assigned courses and failing to appear in their appointed times.'"
8. "'The knowledge of these heavenly signs will be hidden from sinners, leading them to mistakenly worship the stars as deities.'"

9. "'Evil will increase upon the earth, and divine judgment will be executed to bring an end to their wickedness.'"

Chapter 81

1. "'Look upon these celestial tablets, Enoch, and read what is inscribed upon them. Pay close attention to every detail written here.'"
2. "I gazed upon the heavenly tablets and read all that was recorded upon them. I understood their content, which revealed the actions of humanity and the fate of every generation to come."
3. "Immediately, I blessed the great Lord, the King of Glory, for He has created all things. I praised Him for His patience and mercy, and I glorified His name on behalf of humankind."
4. "Then I proclaimed, 'Blessed is the one who dies in righteousness and goodness, for no record of iniquity is kept against him, and he will not face judgment.'"
5. "At that moment, seven holy ones brought me back to the earth and placed me at the entrance of my home. They said to me, 'Tell all these things to your son Methuselah and

instruct your descendants. Teach them that no mortal is without fault before the Lord, for He is their Creator.'"

6. "'You have one more year with Methuselah. Use this time to record all your teachings and to bear witness before your family. After this year, we will take you from the earth.'"
7. "They encouraged me, saying, 'Remain strong, for the righteous will testify to one another. They will rejoice together and praise the Lord in unity.'"
8. "'However, the wicked will perish alongside the wicked, and those who turn away from righteousness will share the fate of others like them.'"
9. "'The righteous will suffer and be taken from the earth because of the deeds of sinners, yet they will be vindicated before the Most High.'"
10. "After they finished speaking, they departed from me. I returned to my people, giving thanks and blessing the Lord of the world."

Chapter 82

1. "Now, my son Methuselah, I have shared everything with you, recording it in writing for your safekeeping. Guard these writings and ensure they are passed down to future generations."
2. "I have imparted wisdom to you and your descendants so that they may pass it on to their children. This wisdom is beyond ordinary understanding."
3. "Those who comprehend it will not tire of learning but will eagerly seek knowledge, for it will nourish them more than the finest food."
4. "Blessed are those who walk in righteousness, for they will not stumble into sin as others do in their days. The sun follows its course across the sky, moving through its portals for thirty days, alongside the stars that guide the year's divisions."
5. "Due to these celestial movements, many will miscalculate the year. However, the luminaries serve as precise indicators, defining a year of exactly 364 days."
6. "People will make errors in counting the days, but these heavenly bodies remain perfectly aligned, with markers placed at the

first, third, fourth, and sixth portals to divide the year into its proper seasons."
7. "The exact length of the year is 364 days. This measurement is precise and unchanging, as revealed to me by Uriel, who is entrusted with the heavenly luminaries."
8. "Uriel governs the cycle of day and night, ensuring the sun, moon, and stars illuminate the world according to their appointed paths."
9. "These are the orders of the stars, each following its designated course, appearing in their correct seasons and cycles under the guidance of their leaders."
10. "Four principal leaders divide the year into its four seasons, accompanied by twelve others who govern the months. Additionally, there are leaders over the thousands of days, and four intercalary days have their own designated overseers to maintain the year's exact divisions."
11. "Among the leaders who divide the year are Milkiel, Helemmelek, Melejal, and Narel."
12. "The secondary leaders include Adnarel, Ijasusael, and Elomeel."
13. "These three follow the main leaders, ensuring the proper stations of the year."

14. "The leader Melkejal rises first at the start of the year, also known as Tamaini, ruling for ninety-one days."
15. "During his time, signs appear: warmth, calm winds, and the flourishing of life. Trees bear fruit, wheat ripens, and the land is covered in vegetation, while winter trees wither."
16. "Under him, the sub-leaders are Berkael, Zelebsel, and Hilujaseph, along with another leader over thousands, named Asfael. When his term ends, the next leader takes over."
17. "Helemmelek, also called 'the shining sun,' follows, ruling for another ninety-one days."
18. "During his period, intense heat and dryness prevail. Fruits ripen, sheep conceive, and the earth yields a full harvest. All produce is gathered, and the winepress is used."
19. "His subordinates are Gidaljal, Keel, and Heel, along with another head of a thousand, named Asfael. His rule concludes at the appointed time."

The Book of Dreams and Visions – Enoch's Ethiopic Book 4

Chapter 83

1. "Now, my son Methuselah, I will recount to you all the visions I have received, narrating them before you."
2. "I had two distinct visions before I took a wife. The first was while I was learning to write, and the second occurred before I married your mother, filling me with fear."
3. "Regarding these visions, I prayed to the Lord. As I lay in my grandfather Mahalalel's house, I saw in a vision the heavens collapsing and falling to the earth."
4. "The ground split open, revealing a vast abyss, while mountains crumbled upon one another, hills collapsed, and towering trees were uprooted and cast down."
5. "A voice entered my mouth, and I cried out, 'The earth is destroyed!'"

6. "My grandfather Mahalalel awoke and asked, 'Why do you cry out, my son? What troubles you?'"
7. "I described my vision to him, and he responded, 'You have seen something of great significance. This dream is a warning of the earth's sins, for destruction will come upon it.'"
8. "He urged me, 'Rise, my son, and make your plea to the Lord of Glory. You have faith—pray that a remnant may be spared so that He does not destroy the entire earth.'"
9. "'For judgment will come from the heavens, and immense devastation will cover the land.'"
10. "So I rose, prayed, and recorded my plea for the generations to come, ensuring that all would know. Then I went outside and observed the sky—the sun rising in the east, the moon setting in the west, the few visible stars, and the earth in its fullness, just as it had been since the beginning. I blessed the Lord of Judgment and praised Him."
11. "He caused the sun to rise from the eastern windows, guiding its path across the sky."

Chapter 84

1. "I lifted my hands in righteousness, offering praise to the Holy and Great One. Using the breath and tongue He has given humanity, I spoke."
2. "He has granted us breath, a voice, and speech, saying, 'Blessed are You, O Lord, the great and mighty King, ruler of all creation in the heavens, the King of kings, and the God of the entire world.'"
3. "Your power, dominion, and majesty endure for all eternity, across every generation. The heavens are Your throne, and the earth Your footstool, now and forever."
4. "You created and govern all things; nothing is beyond Your authority. Wisdom never departs from Your presence, nor does it diminish from Your throne."
5. "You see all, hear all, and nothing is concealed from You, for Your eyes behold everything."
6. "But now, the angels of the heavens have transgressed, and Your wrath is upon humanity until the day of great judgment."
7. "O Sovereign Lord, I implore You—answer my plea. Let a remnant remain on the earth; do not utterly destroy humankind, lest the land be left desolate without inhabitants."

8. "Remove from the world those who have provoked Your wrath, but establish the righteous and upright as an eternal lineage."
9. "Do not turn away from the supplication of Your servant, O Lord."

Chapter 85

1. "After this, I had another vision, which I will recount fully to you, my son."
2. "Enoch raised his voice and spoke to Methuselah, 'Listen, my son, to the words of your father's vision.'"
3. "Before I married your mother, Edna, I saw a vision in my sleep. A great bull emerged from the earth, and it was white."
4. "A heifer followed behind it, accompanied by two bulls—one black and one red."
5. "The black bull attacked the red bull, chasing it across the land until it disappeared from sight."
6. "The black bull grew in strength, while the heifer remained with him. Many oxen were born from him, all resembling him and following in his ways."

7. "The first cow departed from the original bull in search of the red one but could not find him. She lamented bitterly in her search."
8. "Then the first bull returned to comfort her, and her sorrow was eased."
9. "She bore another white bull, from which numerous other bulls and black cows were born."
10. "As I slept, I saw the white bull grow mightier and transform into an enormous white bull. From him emerged many other white bulls, all resembling one another, forming a great assembly."

Chapter 86

1. "While I was asleep, I observed a vision in which a single star fell from the sky and began to move among the oxen, grazing alongside them."
2. "Then I noticed large black oxen, and they all changed their places, pastures, and companions, mingling freely with one another."
3. "Looking up again, I saw many more stars descending from heaven. They joined the

first star, transforming into bulls and integrating with the cattle."

4. "As I watched, these new bulls displayed themselves like horses, mating with the cows among the oxen, leading to conception."

5. "Their offspring were elephants, camels, and donkeys, terrifying the oxen. The new creatures began to attack and consume the oxen, causing chaos."

6. "Fear overtook the inhabitants of the earth, and they fled, trembling in terror at the sight of these monstrous beings."

Chapter 87

1. "I saw how these creatures began fighting and devouring one another, and the earth itself cried out because of their violence."

2. "Lifting my gaze once more to the heavens, I saw a vision of divine beings descending. They appeared as radiant figures, resembling men in white. Four of them arrived first, followed by three others."

3. "The last three took hold of me, lifting me high above the earth so I could observe everything from an elevated position."

4. "One of them said to me, 'Remain here and watch all that happens to the elephants, camels, donkeys, stars, and oxen.'"

Chapter 88

1. "Then I saw one of the four radiant beings seize the fallen star, binding it hand and foot before casting it into a deep abyss, filled with darkness and fearsome depths."
2. "One of the beings took a sword and handed it to the elephants, camels, and donkeys, and suddenly they turned upon each other in fierce battle. The earth trembled as they fought."
3. "As I continued watching, one of the four threw great stones from the heavens upon these creatures. The mighty stars that had joined them, whose bodies resembled horses, were also bound and cast into the depths of the earth."

Chapter 89

1. "One of the four divine beings approached a white bull, revealing a great secret to him in a way that did not cause fear."

2. "The white bull then underwent a transformation, becoming a man, and he proceeded to construct a large vessel for himself."
3. "Three other bulls joined him in the vessel, and they remained inside it, secured from the events outside."
4. "Then I turned my gaze upward and saw a great roof above, from which seven mighty torrents of water flowed down."
5. "These torrents poured with great force, filling an enclosed space with water."
6. "Soon, fountains burst open across the surface of the enclosure, causing the water to rise rapidly."
7. "Before long, the entire area was submerged in water, covered in darkness and mist."
8. "The floodwaters continued to rise, overflowing beyond the enclosure and spreading across the earth."
9. "All the cattle gathered inside the enclosure were caught in the rising waters, and I watched as they were submerged and swallowed by the flood."
10. "Yet, the great vessel remained afloat upon the waters, while the oxen, elephants, camels,

and donkeys were carried away and perished in the depths."
11. "None of them could escape, and they were all lost beneath the floodwaters."
12. "Then, I saw the torrents from above cease, and the earth beneath became stable again."
13. "New channels opened, allowing the water to drain, revealing the land once more."
14. "The great vessel came to rest upon solid ground, and the darkness was replaced with light."
15. "The white bull, now in human form, stepped out of the vessel, accompanied by the three bulls who had been with him."
16. Among the three bulls, one was white, another was red like blood, and the third was black. The white bull separated from them.
17. Then, various creatures emerged, including lions, tigers, wolves, dogs, and other wild animals.
18. In their midst, a white bull was born, and the animals began to attack and bite each other.
19. This white bull fathered a wild ass and another white bull.
20. The wild asses multiplied, while the white bull produced a black wild boar and a white sheep.

21. The wild boars increased in number, and the sheep gave birth to twelve others.
22. As the twelve sheep matured, one was handed over to the asses, who then delivered it to the wolves.
23. This sheep lived among the wolves, but the Lord sent eleven more sheep to join it.
24. Their numbers grew into a large flock, but the wolves oppressed and mistreated them.
25. The wolves feared the sheep, and the sheep cried out to the Lord in their distress.
26. One of the sheep escaped to the wild asses, while the rest cried out with all their might.
27. The Lord, hearing their cries, descended from His high dwelling to care for them.
28. He summoned the escaped sheep and instructed it to warn the wolves to cease their harm against the flock.
29. The sheep, accompanied by another, went to the wolves and delivered the Lord's message.
30. But the wolves continued their oppression, causing the sheep to cry out even louder.
31. Then the Lord arrived in power, striking down the wolves, and they howled in agony.
32. The cries of the sheep ceased as the wolves fled in terror.

33. The sheep moved away from the wolves, but the wolves pursued them relentlessly.
34. The Lord guided His flock, His presence shining with a fearful and glorious light.
35. The wolves chased the sheep to the edge of a vast sea.
36. The waters parted, forming towering walls on both sides, allowing the Lord to lead the sheep through.
37. The wolves hesitated at the sight of the Lord, but when they attempted to follow, the sea closed upon them, drowning them all.
38. Safe from harm, the sheep entered a barren wilderness, devoid of food and water.
39. The Lord provided for them, giving them water and guiding them to green pastures.
40. The sheep that had once led them ascended a high rock, and the Lord sent it back to guide them.
41. The sheep beheld the Lord's majesty and trembled, overwhelmed by His awesome presence.
42. They cried out, saying they could not endure standing before the Lord's glory.
43. The leading sheep climbed the rock once more, while the others began to stray from the path.

44. The Lord became angry at the wandering sheep, prompting the leading one to return from the rock.
45. It found many others blind and lost and began to gather them back into the fold.
46. The strayed sheep, fearing its presence, returned to their places.
47. The leading sheep then transformed into a man and built a dwelling for the Lord of the flock.
48. He placed the sheep within the house, where they lived in peace.
49. The leading sheep eventually passed away, and the flock mourned deeply.
50. As they crossed a stream, two new leaders emerged to guide them.
51. They led the sheep to a fertile land, where the Lord's house was established among them.
52. The sheep sometimes had their eyes opened, yet at other times, they were blind, but another leader arose to bring them back.
53. Wild animals attacked the flock, but the Lord raised a ram to defend them.
54. The ram fought against the beasts but later became proud and oppressive.
55. The Lord appointed another lamb to replace the first ram, making it the leader of the flock.

56. The first ram resisted, chasing the new leader, but the new leader escaped.
57. The dogs attacked and tore down the first ram, and the new leader guided the flock in peace.
58. The flock multiplied and thrived, while the wild beasts withdrew in fear.
59. This leader built a house and a tall tower, which pleased the Lord.
60. Yet again, the flock strayed, and the Lord sent messengers to call them back.
61. But the sheep rejected and killed many of the messengers, with only one escaping to cry out for justice.
62. The Lord of the flock intervened, rescuing the surviving messenger and elevating him.
63. More messengers were sent, but the flock continued to slay them in rebellion.
64. The sheep fell into blindness and abandoned the Lord's house and tower.
65. The Lord permitted lions, tigers, wolves, and foxes to attack and scatter them.
66. The wild beasts ravaged the flock as punishment for their disobedience.
67. In anguish, I cried out for the sheep, but the Lord remained firm in His judgment.

68. Seventy shepherds were appointed to oversee the flock, each given a set number to destroy.
69. The Lord commanded them to tend the flock according to His will, sparing none that He had marked for destruction.
70. An angel was assigned to watch over the shepherds, recording every act of destruction.
71. The shepherds carried out their duties, but they went beyond their orders, destroying more sheep than they had been instructed.
72. Wild beasts also joined in the slaughter, and the Lord's house and tower were reduced to ruins.
73. The shepherds handed the flock over to the wild beasts, and their destruction was recorded.
74. The angel presented the record before the Lord, who read and sealed it.
75. The Lord gazed upon His flock with sorrow, for they had strayed far from Him, but He promised to restore the faithful.
76. Thus, the Lord decreed that those who remained loyal would be gathered once more, and their dwelling would be reestablished in righteousness.

Chapter 90

1. Then I saw in my vision that thirty-five shepherds took turns tending the sheep, each completing their assigned period, just as those before them had done.
2. After them, other shepherds assumed responsibility, taking care of the sheep during their designated times.
3. Then I observed the birds of the sky descending—eagles, vultures, kites, and ravens—all led by the eagles.
4. These birds began attacking the sheep, plucking out their eyes and consuming their flesh.
5. The sheep cried out in pain as they were devoured.
6. In my sleep, I grieved over the shepherds who were supposed to protect the sheep.
7. I saw that the sheep were completely ravaged by dogs, eagles, and kites, until only their bones remained.
8. Their bones fell to the ground, and the number of sheep dwindled.
9. Then, twenty-three more shepherds took over, each fulfilling their assigned time, completing their roles fifty-eight times.

10. Yet amid this destruction, lambs were born among the white sheep, and their eyes began to open.
11. These lambs cried out to the other sheep, but their voices went unheard.
12. The older sheep had become completely deaf, their vision clouded.
13. In the vision, I saw ravens descend upon the lambs, seize one, and tear it apart, devouring it.
14. Then, small horns began to emerge on some of the lambs, but the ravens struck them down.
15. Among the flock, one sheep grew a mighty horn, and its eyes were fully opened.
16. It gazed at the other sheep, calling out to them.
17. The rams noticed it and ran toward it.
18. Meanwhile, the eagles, vultures, ravens, and kites continued their relentless attack on the sheep.
19. Though the sheep remained silent, the rams wailed and cried out in anguish.
20. The ravens attempted to break the great horn of the ram, but they failed.
21. Then, all the birds of prey gathered together,

22. Bringing with them all the sheep of the field, uniting in an effort to destroy the ram's horn.
23. But then, a great sword was given to the sheep, and they rose up against the beasts of the land, slaying them.
24. The wild creatures and birds fled before the sheep.
25. Then, the scribe who had recorded everything under the Lord's command opened the book, revealing the destruction caused by the last twelve shepherds.
26. The record showed that these twelve had brought more ruin than those before them.
27. I watched as the Lord of the sheep came forth, taking in His hand the rod of His wrath and striking the earth.
28. The ground split apart, and all the wild beasts and birds were swallowed by the earth, which then closed over them.
29. Then, a great throne was placed in a fertile land, and the Lord of the sheep sat upon it.
30. The man who had recorded all deeds brought forth the sealed books and opened them before the Lord of the sheep.
31. The Lord summoned the seven first white ones and commanded them to bring forth the

stars that had fallen, whose hidden nature had been like that of horses.

32. These fallen stars were brought before Him.
33. The Lord then instructed the scribe, one of the seven white ones, to bring forth the seventy shepherds who had exceeded their command by destroying more sheep than they had been told to.
34. These shepherds were bound and presented before Him.
35. Judgment was pronounced first upon the stars, and they were found guilty, cast into an abyss of blazing fire.
36. Then, the seventy shepherds were judged, condemned, and thrown into the same fiery abyss.
37. At that moment, another abyss opened upon the earth, filled with flames.
38. The sheep who had been blinded were also judged and found guilty; they, too, were cast into the burning abyss.
39. This fiery chasm was positioned to the right of the Lord's house, and I saw the sheep and their bones consumed by the flames.
40. I stood and watched as the old house was dismantled, its beams, pillars, and decorations carried away.

41. These pieces were taken to a land in the south.
42. Then, the Lord of the sheep established a new house, greater and grander than the first. It was placed where the former house once stood, and all the sheep were gathered within it.

The Epistle of Enoch – The Ethiopic Book of Enoch (Book 5)

Chapter 91

1. "My son Methuselah, gather your brothers and summon all your relatives, for I have important words to share. The Spirit has filled me, and I must reveal what is to come."
2. "Methuselah went out and assembled his brothers and kin, bringing them together."
3. "Then Enoch spoke, saying, 'Listen carefully to your father's words, and heed the wisdom I impart to you. I urge you to embrace righteousness and remain steadfast in it.'"

4. "Stay true to the path of righteousness and do not associate with those who are deceitful in heart. Walk in uprightness, for it will guide you safely, and it will be your trusted companion throughout life."
5. "I see that violence will increase upon the earth, and a great judgment is approaching. Wickedness will be uprooted, and corruption will be completely destroyed."
6. "Once again, evil will multiply—sin, cruelty, and blasphemy will spread, and peace will vanish from the world."
7. "When iniquity reaches its height, judgment will descend from heaven. The Holy One will come in His righteous anger to judge the earth."
8. "In those days, violence will be eradicated, and all evil will be purged from beneath the heavens."
9. "Idolatry and false worship will be cast aside, and every temple built in honor of false gods will be consumed by fire."
10. "Nations will endure fiery judgment and will face the wrath of the Almighty for eternity."
11. "The righteous will awaken, gaining understanding and wisdom."

12. "All roots of wickedness will be removed, and those who have spoken blasphemy will perish by the sword. The rebellious will be wiped out completely."
13. "I urge you to distinguish between the way of righteousness and the path of destruction so that you may fully grasp their consequences."
14. "Choose righteousness, for those who follow evil will meet eternal destruction."

Chapter 92

1. "Enoch's message contains a wisdom that is complete, preserved, and passed down for future generations—those who choose the path of peace and righteousness."
2. "Do not let the times trouble your spirit, for the Almighty has ordained every moment according to His will."
3. "The righteous will rise and walk in truth, and their lives will be filled with goodness and grace."
4. "The Holy One will grant them eternal light and favor, guiding them with His everlasting mercy."
5. "Sin will be cast into darkness, never to return again."

Chapter 93

1. Enoch began to recite from his writings, saying, "I will speak of the children of righteousness, the chosen ones of the earth, and the plant of righteousness that will never wither."
2. "I was born in the seventh generation, in a time when righteousness and justice still thrived among men."
3. "In the second generation, deception spread, leading to the first great judgment, yet one righteous individual was spared."
4. "During the third, a chosen one emerged, and his descendants carried righteousness forward for generations."
5. "In the fourth, holy ones received visions, and a divine law was established for all who would follow it."
6. "In the fifth, an everlasting house of glory was constructed, where righteousness would dwell."
7. "The sixth era saw wisdom fade, and the people became blind to the truth."
8. "In the seventh, an apostate generation arose, steeped in great unrighteousness and corruption."

9. "At the end of this time, the chosen righteous ones will receive sevenfold wisdom regarding the mysteries of creation."

Chapter 94

1. "My children love righteousness and follow it, for the ways of righteousness are worthy of pursuit, while the paths of wickedness lead only to destruction."
2. "There will be some who teach the ways of death and ruin, but the righteous must separate themselves from such people."
3. "Do not choose the ways of wrongdoing, for those who do will meet their downfall."
4. "Instead, seek after righteousness and a life of peace, so that you may flourish and prosper."
5. "Hold fast to my words and let them remain in your hearts, for I know that sinners will try to lead you astray from wisdom."
6. "Woe to those who build their lives on deception, for their schemes will collapse, leaving them without peace."

7. "Woe to those who establish their security through evil, for they will fall by the sword of judgment."
8. "Woe to the wealthy who put their trust in riches, forgetting the Most High."
9. "Because of their wickedness, they prepare themselves for the day of reckoning and ultimate destruction."
10. "I tell you: The One who created you will overthrow you; He will show no mercy in your downfall, and your ruin will not be met with pity."
11. "In those days, the righteous will stand as a reproach to the sinners and the ungodly."

Chapter 95

1. "Oh, that my eyes were like the clouds heavy with rain, that I might weep for you, shedding endless tears to ease my sorrow for what is to come!"
2. "Who allowed you to become so steeped in wickedness and shame? Judgment will soon be upon you!"
3. "Fear not, you who are righteous, for the Lord will deliver the sinners into your hands for judgment."

4. "Woe to those who speak curses that cannot be undone; there will be no healing for you because of your transgressions."
5. "Woe to you who repay good with evil, for you will be repaid in full for your deeds."
6. "Woe to those who bear false witness and commit injustice, for your end will come swiftly."
7. "Woe to you, sinners, for you will be pursued for your wrongdoings, and the burden of your guilt will be too heavy to bear."

Chapter 96

1. "Take heart, O righteous, for soon the sinners will collapse, and you will rise above them."
2. "In their downfall, your children will soar like eagles, lifting themselves high above the turmoil."
3. "You will find refuge in the hidden places of the earth and seek shelter among the rocks, while the wicked lament their fate."
4. "Do not be afraid, for healing and light will be yours, and a voice from heaven will bring you comfort."

5. "Woe to those who are deceived by wealth, believing themselves to be just, for their own hearts will bear witness against them."
6. "Woe to those who exploit the weak and live in excess, for they will come to nothing."
7. "Woe to those who turn away from the source of life, for they will be consumed in destruction."
8. "Woe to the powerful who oppress the righteous, for the day of their ruin is near."

Chapter 97

1. "O righteous ones, know that the sinners will be disgraced and will perish in the time of their wrongdoing."
2. "Be warned, O sinners, for the Most High has not overlooked your judgment, and even the angels rejoice in your downfall."
3. "What will you do, O transgressors, and where will you hide on the day of reckoning when you hear the cries of the righteous?"
4. "You will be counted among those condemned, for you have walked in the ways of wickedness."

5. "In that hour, the prayers of the just will reach the Lord, and the days of your punishment will begin."
6. "Every act of evil you have done will be revealed before the Great Holy One, and you will stand in disgrace as He rejects all the works built on corruption."
7. "Woe to you who live by the land and sea, for your memory is stained with iniquity."
8. "Woe to those who hoard silver and gold through dishonest gain, saying, 'We have wealth and lack nothing.'"
9. "Yet your riches will vanish like water slipping through your fingers, for they were gathered through wickedness, and a heavy curse awaits you."

Chapter 98

1. "I swear to you, both the wise and the foolish, that you will witness astonishing things on the earth."
2. "Men will clothe themselves in finery like women, adorning themselves with bright garments, as though they were kings. They will revel in power, wealth, and splendor, yet their lives will pour out like water."

3. "In their vanity, wisdom will abandon them, and they will perish in disgrace, their riches leading them to destruction and ruin. Their spirits will be cast into the flames."
4. "I declare to you, sinners, just as mountains cannot become slaves, nor hills servants, sin was not created by the earth. It was mankind who brought it forth, and those who embrace it will be cursed."
5. "A woman was not meant to be barren, yet through her own ways, she may pass without children."
6. "I swear by the Great Holy One that every wicked act you commit is known in the heavens; no deed of oppression is concealed."
7. "Do not deceive yourselves into thinking you go unnoticed, for every sin is recorded daily before the Most High."
8. "Be certain that all your injustices are written down, and you are prepared for the day of destruction."
9. "Woe to you who are foolish, for your own folly will be your downfall. You rebel against the wise, yet prosperity will not be yours."
10. "Know this: you are marked for a day of ruin. Do not hope for life, O sinners, for you will pass away without ransom."

11. "Woe to you, whose hearts are hardened in wickedness and violence. You partake of the blessings the Most High provides, yet peace will not be granted to you."
12. "Woe to those who take pleasure in the suffering of the righteous, for no resting place will be given to you."
13. "Woe to those who reject the words of the just, for eternal life will not be yours."
14. "Woe to those who spread falsehoods and ungodly speech, leading others to commit evil against their neighbors."
15. "Because of this, you will never know peace, and destruction will come upon you suddenly."

Chapter 99

1. "Woe to those who indulge in wickedness and take pride in their deceit, for they will perish without joy."
2. "Woe to those who twist the words of righteousness, violate the eternal laws, and turn toward corruption; they will be trampled upon the earth."
3. "In those days, O righteous ones, lift your voices in prayer as a testimony before the

angels, so they may bring the sins of the wicked before the Most High."
4. "The nations will be shaken, and all the families of the earth will rise on the day of destruction."
5. "Mothers will abandon their infants, even the nursing ones, leaving them to perish without mercy."
6. "I swear to you, O sinners, that an unending day of bloodshed is destined for you because of your transgressions."
7. "Those who bow to idols and serve spirits will find no refuge in them."
8. "They will turn away from truth, consumed by fear and ignorance, and will swiftly meet their demise for their false worship."
9. "Blessed are those who seek wisdom and righteousness, for they will not fall among the lawless; they will be delivered."
10. "Woe to those who bring harm to their neighbors; they will descend into the abyss."
11. "Woe to those who spread deception across the earth; they will be consumed by their own schemes."
12. "Woe to those who build wealth through the suffering of others and construct their homes

with ill-gotten gain; peace will flee from them."
13. "Woe to those who abandon the inheritance of their ancestors and chase after false gods; they will find no rest."
14. "Woe to those who practice oppression and afflict their fellow men; the day of reckoning is near."
15. "The Lord will bring down your arrogance, fill your hearts with sorrow, and turn all your glory to ruin. The righteous will remember your sins."

Chapter 100

1. "On that day, fathers and sons will fall together, and brothers will strike each other down, staining the rivers with their blood."
2. "The wicked will have no restraint, shedding blood from sunrise to sunset."
3. "Horses will wade through the blood of sinners, and chariots will be drenched in it."
4. "In that time, the angels will descend to gather those who led others into sin, and the Most High will judge them alongside the unrighteous."

5. "The righteous will be shielded by the holy angels, cherished like precious treasures, and though they rest in death, they will have no fear."
6. "The wise will dwell in peace, and understanding will grow, for the riches of the sinful will not preserve them when they fall."
7. "Woe to you, O sinners, in the time of great distress! You have oppressed the righteous and tormented them with fire; now you will receive your due reward."
8. "Woe to you who harden your hearts and plot evil; terror will strike you, and no one will come to your aid."
9. "Woe to you, O lawless ones, for your wickedness will ignite a fire that burns hotter than any flame."
10. "The sun, moon, and stars will bear witness against you, for you have condemned the innocent without cause."
11. "The clouds, mist, and rain will testify against you, withholding their gifts from you."
12. "You will offer bribes to summon the rain, but your wealth will be worthless."
13. "When frost, snow, and storms strike, you will not endure."

Chapter 101

1. "Look up, O children of the heavens, and observe the mighty works of the Most High. Stand in awe of Him and turn away from evil."
2. "If He seals the heavens and holds back the rain and dew because of your sins, what will you do then?"
3. "If His wrath is poured out upon you for your iniquities, how will you plead when you have spoken so arrogantly against Him?"
4. "Know this: peace will flee from you."
5. "Look at those who sail the seas, how their ships are tossed by the waves, filling their hearts with fear."
6. "They dread the ocean and its dangers, yet you sinners show no fear of the Most High, who made both the sea and the dry land."
7. "Do not the sailors tremble before the mighty waters? Yet you, O sinners, have no reverence for the Creator who set its boundaries."
8. "The heavens and the earth were formed by His command, and He granted wisdom to all living things."

9. "Yet despite His marvelous works, you who live in sin do not fear Him."

Chapter 102

1. "When the time comes for a consuming fire to descend upon you, where will you flee? Where will you find refuge?"
2. "When His judgment is spoken against you, will you not be filled with dread?"
3. "The very stars will tremble, and the earth will quake beneath His mighty hand."
4. "You, O sinners, will be cursed for eternity, forever without peace."
5. "But you, righteous ones, do not be afraid. Hold onto hope, even in death, if you have lived in righteousness."
6. "Do not mourn when your soul descends to Sheol, for your goodness will not go unrewarded."
7. "When you pass away, the wicked may mock and say, 'The righteous die just as we do, gaining nothing from their virtue.'"
8. "But I tell you, sinners, though you live in pleasure and sin without fear, your end will be far different from the righteous."

9. "The righteous may suffer in death, but their spirits will endure,
10. "While you, O sinners, will suffer torment in Sheol forever."

Chapter 103

1. "Now, I make a solemn oath to you, O righteous ones, by the glory of the Almighty who reigns over all. I unveil to you a profound mystery.
2. "I have read the sacred writings recorded in the heavens, the holy books inscribed on high. Within them, I discovered the truth about those who have passed away in righteousness."
3. "They are promised joy, honor, and a great reward for their deeds on earth—blessings that exceed those given to the living."
4. "The spirits of the righteous, though no longer among men, will rejoice before the Most High, and their remembrance will never fade but endure eternally."
5. "Do not be troubled by the scorn of the wicked, for your place is secure before the Holy One."

6. "Woe to those who die in sin, leaving behind the wealth they accumulated through unrighteousness. Though people may say, 'Blessed are those who prospered in sin,'
7. "Even if they depart from this world in wealth and honor, their souls will descend to the depths, where judgment and torment await them."
8. "They will be cast into darkness, bound in chains, and consumed by flames, where suffering continues from generation to generation. "Woe to you, sinners, for peace will never be yours."
9. "Do not say of the righteous, 'We have toiled in vain, endured hardship, and suffered greatly while wickedness thrived around us.'
10. "'We were crushed under the weight of injustice, abandoned with no help, persecuted, and left in despair."
11. "We sought to lead, yet we were made servants. We humble ourselves before the wicked, but they showed no kindness, nor did they provide shelter for us.'
12. "'They supported those who plundered and scattered us, disregarding their own guilt against the righteous.'"

Chapter 104

1. "I assure you, righteous ones, by the holy angels above: Your names are eternally written before the Great One."
2. "Every deed you have done and every hardship you have endured is recorded in the presence of the Mighty One."
3. "Take heart, for though you have suffered disgrace, you will shine like the stars in the sky. The gates of heaven will be open for you."
4. "Call upon justice, and it will be granted to you. Those who have oppressed you will face judgment before the Most High."
5. "Hold fast to your hope, O righteous ones."
6. "A time of great joy awaits, as the angels in heaven rejoice over you. Why should you fear the day of judgment? You will not be numbered among the wicked."
7. "That day of judgment is reserved for those who have strayed from righteousness, from every generation."
8. "Do not be troubled by the success of sinners, nor follow in their ways."

9. "Keep yourselves separate from their cruelty and injustice, for you are companions of the heavenly beings."
10. "Even if the wicked claim, 'No one will discover our sins, nor will they be remembered,' know that every act is recorded daily."
11. "The Great One who sees all keeps account of light and darkness, day and night, as witnesses to every action."
12. "Do not let godlessness enter your hearts. Speak truthfully and never accuse the Holy One of injustice."
13. "Do not place your trust in false gods, for deception and irreverence lead to wrongdoing. I reveal this mystery: the wicked will alter the words of truth, spreading falsehoods and composing deceitful writings."
14. "Yet, when my words are finally written truthfully, without distortion or omission, a new revelation will be made known."
15. "Sacred writings will be given to the wise and just, bringing them joy, understanding, and righteousness."
16. "The righteous will embrace these words, rejoice in them, and walk in the path of truth.

Those who follow these teachings will receive their reward, for they have chosen the way of justice."

Chapter 105

1. "At that time, the Lord will instruct the righteous to testify to their wisdom. Their reward for guiding the earth will be revealed."
2. "I, along with My Son, will dwell among them forever, leading in the ways of righteousness. You, the children of truth, will find everlasting joy and peace. Amen."

Chapter 106

1. "After some time, my son Methuselah arranged a marriage for his son Lamech, and in due time, his wife gave birth to a child."
2. "The newborn had skin as white as snow, with a radiant glow, and his hair was like pure wool."
3. "His eyes shone brilliantly, and when he opened them, the entire house was illuminated as if the sun itself had risen within it."

4. "The child immediately praised the Lord of righteousness."
5. "Overcome with fear, Lamech hurried to his father, Methuselah, and said, 'I have fathered an unusual child, unlike any human I have seen.'"
6. "'His appearance is extraordinary, almost divine, and I fear he may not be of my lineage but instead a being from the angels.'"
7. "'Father, I beg you, go to Enoch, who dwells among the holy ones, and inquire about this child to learn the truth.'"
8. "Hearing Lamech's plea, Methuselah set out to find me at the farthest reaches of the earth. He called my name, and I heard his voice."
9. "I went to meet him and asked, 'What brings you here, my son?'"
10. "Methuselah answered, 'I am troubled by a vision and the birth of an unusual child in my son Lamech's household.'"
11. "'The child's appearance is unlike any other; his skin is white as snow, his eyes shine like the sun, and his hair is like wool.'"
12. "I, Enoch, replied, 'The Lord is about to bring forth a great event upon the earth.'"

13. "'The angels have transgressed by taking human wives and producing giant offspring.'"
14. "'Because of this corruption, a great judgment is destined to come upon the world.'"
15. "'A mighty flood will cleanse the earth, but this child will be spared.'"
16. "'Tell Lamech to name him Noah, for he will be the one who survives.'"
17. "'Through Noah, a new generation will rise, and the earth will be repopulated after the destruction.'"

Chapter 107

1. "I read on the sacred tablets of heaven that generation after generation would continue in their wrongdoing until the appointed time of righteousness would come. On that day, all forms of wickedness will be wiped away, and sin will vanish from the earth, leaving only purity and goodness to remain."
2. "Now, my son, return to Lamech and assure him that this child is truly his own—there is no deception in this matter."
3. "When Methuselah heard these words from his father Enoch, who had revealed these

hidden truths, he went back to Lamech. Lamech named the child Noah, saying, 'This one will bring relief to the earth after the great calamity that is to come.'"

Chapter 108

1. "This is another message that Enoch recorded for his son Methuselah and for those who would live in the final days, remaining faithful to the divine law."
2. "'You who have walked in righteousness, stand firm and await the day when the end will come for those who embrace wickedness. The fall of the mighty who transgress is inevitable.'"
3. "'Be patient as sin is erased, for the names of the unrighteous will be removed from the book of life and from the sacred records. Their legacy will be utterly destroyed.'"
4. "'Their spirits will be severed, and they will cry out in agony in a barren desolation, suffering in unrelenting flames without rest or relief.'"
5. "I saw a vast cloud, deep and impenetrable, with an intense fire burning within it, while radiant mountains flickered and moved across its expanse."

6. "I turned to one of the holy angels standing beside me and asked, 'What is this brilliant and consuming fire? It is not the dwelling place of the righteous, yet it burns with immense fury.'"
7. "The angel responded, 'This is where the spirits of sinners and those who blaspheme are cast. It is the place of torment for those who have distorted the words of the prophets and led others astray.'"
8. "Their actions are recorded in the heavens so that the angels may bear witness and understand the judgment awaiting the wicked."
9. "Among them, however, are also the souls of the humble and just—those who have endured great suffering in their earthly lives. Their reward will be immense."
10. "These individuals were scorned and humiliated by the wicked, yet they never sought worldly riches. They remained steadfast, recognizing the fleeting nature of earthly existence."
11. "The Lord tested them, refining their spirits to prove their purity, so that they might bring glory to His name. Their blessings are eternally inscribed in the heavenly records."

12. "Despite being oppressed and mistreated, they chose to honor My name rather than seek earthly vengeance or gain."
13. "I will call forth the righteous spirits from among the children of light. Those who were once hidden in darkness, denied recognition for their faith, will be glorified. They will be brought into the presence of divine light, seated on thrones of honor, shining eternally in radiance. In His righteous judgment, God will reward them abundantly. The righteous will witness the fate of those who lived in darkness, cast into eternal suffering, never to escape.
14. The condemned will wail in anguish as they see the righteous bathed in glory, while they themselves are hurled into an abyss of never-ending torment."

www.ingramcontent.com/pod-product-compliance
Lightning Source LLC
LaVergne TN
LVHW051604070426
835507LV00021B/2769